I Hate
New Music

I Hate New Music

THE CLASSIC ROCK MANIFESTO

BY DAVE THOMPSON

Backbeat
Books

An Imprint of Hal Leonard Corporation

New York

Published in 2008 by Backbeat Books
An Imprint of Hal Leonard Corporation
7777 West Bluemound Road
Milwaukee, WI 53213

Trade Book Division Editorial Offices
19 West 21st Street, New York, NY 10010

The Lurkers, "Come and Reminisce," from the CD *Fried Brains*. Written by Arturo Bassick, published by Captain Oi! Music. Lyrics used courtesy of Captain Oi!

Printed in the United States of America

Book design by Mark Bergeron

Library of Congress Cataloging-in-Publication Data is available upon request.

ISBN 978-0-87930-935-0

www.backbeatbooks.com

To K-Mart (not the store!) and Sassy

Nostalgia is a lot of fun
Now that I've turned 51
If it's new I won't go,
They won't play a thing I know
The missus thinks it's no good
I've got my second childhood
I won't even buy new stuff
By the bands I used to love

—The Lurkers, "Come and Reminisce"

Contents

Contents

FOREWORD

Jethro Tull Slept Here

IRST THINGS FIRST. Unless there's a pressing need, like say (f'rinstance) you're genuinely psychotic, or, less likely, in the thrall of an actual inspiration or idea (other than "glory," other than "scoring"), nobody should be wasting his/her sacred/profane oo-poo-pa-doo playing rock-a-roll no more: NOBODY, y'hear? It's about as necessary—as opposed to culturally, carnally *mandatory*—as making papier-mâché John Malkovich masks or dropping a dump each morning in the eighteenth hole of your neighborhood miniature golf course.

Once upon a merry time, it probably was needed, needed *baaaad*, but that was before rock-roll was EVERYWHERE—back when you didn't hear it in supermarkets, 24/7, or over the phone waiting to speak with a dental receptionist, or blasting at you from every SUV on Main Street, or fueling the steroidal swagger of World Wrestling Federation dipwads—before "rock-surround" was our eternal condition.

What we need now is to *turn it off*. What was once liberating has become irredeemably oppressive, existing solely and wholly to make us all stoooopid, Jack—just like cop shows or elections or college football . . . or our fucking PARENTS, for cryin' out loud.

Before any of you start a band, or join a band, or aid or abet a band, it is better by far that you pump gas for sub-sub-minimum wage, fish pennies out of port-a-pots at NASCAR hoedowns, change the deep fat at White Castle, go back to school for a degree in pus farming, or poke an ice pick through your tongue.

If, in spite of such warning, by some tragic mischance, you should find yerself IN a band, no studio big or small would be right to record its sonic upchuck, nor any entrepreneur scrupulous or unto press, release, market, or exploit it, and no writer, pro or am, should under ANY CIRCUMSTANCES play naive onlooker and scribble liner notes, Hall of Fame induction rants, or biographic pictobooks for the coffee trays and crappers of the world. No, no, NOOOOOOOOOOO!

Additionally, subtractionally, and moreover, any scribbler who would willfully reinforce the resulting house-o-cards by shilling for bands, many or any, from a theoretically rooty-toot PAST should be flogged, and those cheesy enough to compose so-called histories, be they hoss-shit from the git-go, heinous revisionism, or the uncircumcised "truth," should be dumped head-foist down a deep well in Belgium.

That said, I, the none too shabby R*i*c*h*a*r*d M*e*l*t*z*e*r, aka Borneo Jimmy, rockrooter emeritus, originator of the whole sorry rockroot shuck, herewith endorse the LONE EXCEPTION to any and all of the above: the one, the only *I Hate New Music*.

Hate New Music!

New!! Music!!!

Hate it!!!

Dig it, folks: The tome you hold, *I Hate New Music: The Classic Rock Manifesto* by Dave Thompson (not to be confused with Dennis Thompson, Hunter Thompson, or David Thomas) is the flying fucking SHIT!

And why's that?

Because.

Because what?

Just because.

AWRIGHT!!!!!

—RICHARD MELTZER,
winner of the 2006 Hoppenploptop Award

Welcome to the Future

A LITTLE OVER A CENTURY AGO, during the Sioux Wars of the 1870s, my great-grandmother was one of a handful of gallant ladies recruited by the US Army to entertain the troops. A precursor of the traveling bands of performers who were so vital to military morale through subsequent 130 years worth of wars, Granny and the girls would travel by creaky steam locomotive across miles of hostile territory, to sing and dance for the soldiers before the next day's battle.

Two decades later, America was again at war, this time with Spain, and Granny was again in the thick of the action. But something had changed in the intervening years: *Granny* had changed. At the Battle of Little Big Horn, the troops could not get enough of her. She kicked her legs, they roared for more. She shook her tush, they screamed for an encore. Twenty-five years later, at the Battle of San Juan Hill, all they did was beg for mercy. She was too old to be showing so much leg, too wrinkly to be waving her ass in the air. Without putting too fine a point on it, she was Past It.

I never knew Granny, but I know all about her. A trouper to the last, she refused to call it quits. Come the next war, the Great War, she packed up the glass where she kept her false teeth, her walking frame, and a few tins of cat food, and decamped for France, to twirl in the trenches.

It was there, in a last desperate attempt to give our boys a morale-boosting lift, that she developed her greatest stunt yet: juggling with live hand grenades. Official army records claim the 23rd Platoon (Unmounted) was destroyed by friendly fire in December 1917. There was no such thing as friendly fire—they were wiped out by a senile old bat who wouldn't admit she was finished.

No, I never knew Granny, but I could not help thinking of her recently, whilst attending Ozzfest.

Oswald Osbourne, the gentleman after whom the festival is named, has a lot in common with Granny. Both began their careers in their early twenties: Granny in 1869, in church every Sabbath; Oswald precisely one century later, in a group called Black Sabbath. While granny played the Big Horn, Oswald played the big stadia. Granny rode the iron horse; Oswald sang of Iron Man. Both said the stage was in their blood; both were unable to ever bring down the curtain.

"Never say die," sang Oswald on his final album with Black Sabbath. "Don't you ever say die. No. Don't." Musically, the composition was a little weak, and nowhere near as good as, say, "Supernaut," but the sentiment was admirable. Granny would have loved it, anyway.

There, however, the parallels seem to end. When Granny went back on the road, a year shy of fifty and, quite frankly, looking a lot worse for wear, the people who once loved her jeered. "Get back to your knitting!" they cried. "Don't you have a bingo game to go to?" Oswald, on the other hand, more cheered and applauded, treated like a king, worshipped by people more than half his age.

Ordinarily, one would assume this to be a good thing. Talent does not, as a rule, dry up and blow away because one has passed one of those magic milestones that society insists on appending to the passing years—thirty, forty, fifty. Many late-blooming boomers will tell you they feel no different today than they did the last time they turned thirty-nine, and the sound track to the Rolling Stones' Martin Scorsese movie sounds as fierce today as any other concert recording they've released since *Get Yer Ya Yas Out*.

Similarly, it can only be a cause for celebration that the cult of rampant ageism, which once ran riot through the world of rock 'n' roll, passed away around the same time as its leading progenitors passed their sixtieth birthdays. Peter Townshend, for example, is probably rather glad he didn't die before he got old; he'd have missed the last twenty years if he had, and then where would the Who be? A one-man band, and Roger Daltrey's already written off one solo career.

At the same time, is there not something extraordinarily undignified about the sight of a somewhat-later-than-middle-aged man—and that is being generous—still hauling himself around a stage, belting out songs that he wrote in the first flush of youth, rekindling the excitement he felt as a child?

In other professions—accountancy, for example, or real estate—a fifty-nine-year-old suddenly reverting to the sallow-faced brat he left behind forty years before would be held up for ridicule, mocked by his peers, and probably consigned to a lifetime of psychiatric counseling. Even in the arts, age confers a dignity one cannot resist. Actress Susan Sarandon got her start in *The Rocky Horror Show*, but could you imagine her doing the Time Warp today?

Then there is Granny, who learned in the worst possible way that singing and dancing should be left to the youngsters. It is quite permissible to grow old gracefully. But few people actually remain graceful as they grow old.

Why is rock 'n' roll any different? Oswald Osbourne, Robert Dylan, Michael Jagger, Ignatius Pop—mere months now separate them from pensionable status, if they have not already passed it. To paraphrase Charles Dickens, do they have no lawns to mow? Wills to write? Are there no jigsaws? No community centers? Or is this really how we treat our old folk these days, expecting them to prostitute the last remnants of their youthful talent for the sniggering amusement of a few thousand vicarious voyeurs, the same kind of hooligan tearaways who laugh when an old lady trips over her walker in the supermarket, or who make jokes about their grandparents smelling of boiled cabbage.

I do not know whether Oswald Osbourne smells of boiled cabbage. I do not know whether he has ever tripped in a supermarket. I do not even know which side of the bed he prefers to keep his teeth on. But I do know that he is entitled to some respect in his dotage—respect and the chance to enjoy his retirement in the same relaxed fashion that you or I would hope to. That means he should be out in the garden, not playing the Garden: He is not a performing seal; he is not a circus clown; and it is unforgivable that modern youth—polluted by that irreverent, mocking mind set which is so prevalent these days—should expect him to become either of these. Yes, I attended Ozzfest, and though I sympathized with Mr. Osbourne's plight, I still felt guilty for being there. And in your own heart of hearts, I expect you do as well.

I Hate
New Music

Is That a Bustle in Your Hedgerow? or, Are You Just Pleased to See Me?

In which we commence to plan a road map of where music has been, and where it all went so horribly wrong. And it only mentions Bon Jovi once, so you're all right, because you're already past it.

BACK IN THE DAYS WHEN ROCK WAS ROCK, and Asia was a place where odd-looking pressings of Led Zeppelin albums you'd never heard of came from, you could walk into a record store and know you weren't going to be mortally offended by whatever was spinning on the counter clerk's turntable. Because they didn't call them counter clerks in those days. They were simply the guy (or the girl) at the record store, and they were your friend and ally, before you'd ever met them.

"Hey, man, how ya doing?"

"Fine."

"Can I help you find anything?"

"Ah, I was just wondering if anything new has come in?"

And they'd look you up and down, clock your tastes from the length of your hair and the cut of your clothes, and reel off half a dozen things that you really needed to hear.

Today, some bored little cow with half an ironmonger's store stuck through her cheeks will glance disdainfully over and say, "I don't know," then get back to whatever she was doing before you walked in and disturbed her with your dumb questions.

It was a time when buying two tickets for a concert didn't necessitate uploading your Social Security number and three biometric samples to a remote server in the Crimea.

An age when you handed somebody some money and they gave you a piece of plastic in a cardboard sleeve, with lyrics and liner notes and a real neat picture. Not a microscopic computer file that you can only play through your tinny laptop speakers, and it still sounds like shit that's been run over with a forklift truck.

A day when you could open the latest issue of *Rotting Stone* or *Spit* and stand a chance of having actually heard of whichever band was that week sounding off on a subject that they knew nothing about. Like the annoying one from Fall Out Boy standing up to say he doesn't think that saving the Earth has anything to do with politics. Too many words, matey. You don't think. Full stop.

And an era when genuinely lasting reputations were made with single moments of majesty, as opposed to videos that would be forgotten before the end of the next commercial break. A time when you actually looked forward to hearing a new album by a piano-playing singer-songwriter, as opposed to hiding in the corner until it was over.

Think about that for a moment. Remember the first time you ever heard "Saturday Night's Alright (for Fighting)" and, in the razor-blade slash of that manic guitar, you witnessed the utter deconstruction of Elton John's past renown as a mellow singer-songwriter with a penchant for toe-curling doggerel and songs about his penis. Especially when he followed through with "Bennie and the Jets."

Now remember the first time you heard . . . oh, what's-her-name, the fluffy-haired bint who was on MTV once, with a song about how her boyfriend didn't want to have sex with her on a Saturday because it interfered with lunch with his web designer. As if we care. I'm fortysomething, you're twentyblah. Come back when you've got some living behind you and your world has stopped revolving around a succession of manufactured crises involving whose turn it is to use the Hello Kitty vibrator this week and how much time you spent at rehab. Real rockers don't go to rehab. Real rockers don't even know what rehab is, and if you tried to tell them they'd rip your fucking head off and snort your brains out with a straw.

Oh, and don't try wriggling out of it by pointing out that most of the albums *I* like were made by people just as young as you. Van Morrison was twenty-four when he recorded *Astral Weeks*; Neil Young made *After the Gold Rush* at twenty-five. So what? Forty years on, people are still singing "Only Love Can Break Your Heart." Four days on and I can't even remember the name of your current "hit."

But we are wandering. Elton John. "Saturday Night's Alright (for Fighting)." People don't make records like that any more because people don't *do* things like that anymore. They don't take chances, they don't challenge their audiences, they don't even write songs about their penises.

Yes, bands will take an allegedly unexpected bodyswerve in the middle of their career and kick all their past doings into the trash can, but it's not the same thing, and it's certainly not for the same reasons.

Elton and his musical convolutions were important because he continued making his old-style music even as he marched forward with the new. For every "Saturday Night's Alright (for Fighting)," there was a "Goodbye Yellow Brick Road." For every "Jamaica Jerkoff" there was a "Grey Seal." He was consistent and, at least until he went rubbish in the mid-'70s, he was consistently good.

Today bands have to keep changing because they take so long between new records that whatever style of music they were making five years ago, the last time they stirred off their asses, probably doesn't even exist any longer.

"Van Morrison's first album in over a year!" proclaimed *Rolling Stone* in its review of *Moondance* in 1970. Over a year! Can you imagine? Today, even the hottest young things take two or three years between new releases, and that's if they're rushed into it, or think they have something urgent to impart (like a tale of just getting out of rehab). Between summer 1968 and spring 1970, on the other hand, the Steve Miller Band released five new LPs, an average of one every five months. Modern would-be mavericks the White Stripes have been recording since 1999 and they've still only issued six albums.

Miller explained, "It takes so long, and so much work to get into the space to write that kind of stuff, that once you're there you really want to be as productive as you can. I learned that from the Beatles; I was astounded by how much great material they had in the can that hadn't been released. They were the first artists I ever met that were ahead of [things] instead of behind, and I thought, you know, ahead is a lot better than behind."

Today, Miller continued, "you're Nirvana, you just sold eleven million records, where's your next album? The public, which is huge and wants it, has to wait for three years, and by then half of them have forgotten about you." And the other half have moved onto other pleasures.

Time moved slower in the past, or maybe life moved faster. Record companies didn't need to spend more time plotting the promotional campaign than a band took to record an album. The final mix on the Beatles' eponymous "white album" was completed just one month before the record hit the stores. The final mix on the latest offering from This Year's Hot New Bubonic Plagiarist could have been done at any time in the last year, and the only difference between the two is, *The Beatles* is still being listened to forty years later. One doubts whether more than half a dozen of the albums released this year will even be remembered past Christmas.

You could say it's a generational thing. There were fewer distractions in "ye olden dayes," less twenty-four-hour bombardment from every media that can raise its voice, less Internet porn to drool over when you should be writing a song, and a lot less music being thrown at us.

But that does not necessarily mean that there was more good music. Every era has its heroes, but it also has its villains and, if we look at the biggest names of the early to mid-1970s, the Osmonds, the Partridge Family, the Carpenters, Abba, and John Denver scream as loudly as any that you might deliberately remember. The Bay City Rollers, the Starland Vocal Band, the Bellamy Brothers. Look at it in those terms, and it's a wonder that we even survived.

But we did, and here's why: It's the Elton John principle again. For every Tony Orlando and Dawn, there was an Ozark Mountain Daredevils. For every "Seasons in the Sun" there was a "Panama Red." Today? Coldplay is Travis is Muse is the Stereophonics, and the only thing that differentiates any of them is the speed with which one can rewrite what the other just did. Music was once delineated in shades of gray. Today, it is strictly black and white. Their last album was soft, their new one is hard, and look how they've developed as *artistes*. But it has nothing to do with development and even less to do with artistry. Music is about singing the songs of your spirit. It is not a race, it is not a competition, it is not the Super Bowl. We don't care how clever you are. We want to know how much soul you have. And the answer is . . . none. You wouldn't be making your career in the twenty-first-century music industry if you did.

We return to the chalkboard. There are threads to follow here, both historical and musical. When Free broke up, vocalist Paul Rodgers formed Bad Company with Mott the Hoople's Mick Ralphs and, for a time, Rodgers continued with business as usual. It all got a little predictable after a while, because there are only so many times that you can rewrite "Feel Like Making Love" and pretend that you're making a major new statement. But at least you'd written the song in the first place and weren't simply knocking out a knockoff because your own imagination was stifled at birth.

Foghat spun out of one of Savoy Brown leader Kim Simmonds' regular membership purges and brought a whole new life force to a British blues ferment that never seemed to grow old. They, too, grew preposterous in the end, a parody of a cliché that was emulating a spoof. But again, at least it was a spoof of their own creation. Unlike, say, a band like Franz Ferdinand, whose greatest musical accomplishment so far would appear to be *not* being sucked out into space because their music has so little atmosphere. Besides, how many times can you listen to a band that believes guitars should sound like a spastic jerking off.

People have always been influenced by others. The Rolling Stones might never have existed if the American blues hadn't written their first three albums for them. John Lennon would still be cropping shares on the Mersey Delta if Lonnie Donegan hadn't invented skiffle. And when jolly Joe Walsh left the James Gang, no sooner had he finished showcasing a new vocal-guitar effect called the talk box (during "Rocky Mountain High") than Peter Frampton was taking the same device to the top of the charts via "Show Me the Way."

The difference is, Frampton (and the Stones and the Beatles) wasn't copying. He was creating, and, close to twenty million copies later, one only needs to hear the lad take the breath that ignites the gargle to be transported to an alternate reality where *every* record is that amazing. It might have sounded like he was drowning sheep, but "Show Me the Way" is still as spellbinding today, when he's all bald and shiny, as it was when he had a headful of swoonworthy curls.

Will we be saying the same thing in another thirty years' time about Mars Volta and Goldfrapp? Will there be a new edition of this book on the shelves in 2040, looking back at the classic rock of the early twenty-first century, demanding to know why nobody in mid-century music makes records as great as the Libertines used to, or how the now-geriatric Kaiser Chiefs' latest live album proves they are still as vibrant as they were when they were kids?

Maybe they will. People can be funny about their pasts, because every one of us grows up in a golden age of some sort, where the music's always better and the TV's always smarter, and our sports team was at its most brilliantly scintillating.

Most of the time, they are right as well. When I was twelve, David Bowie was Ziggy Stardust, Katy Manning was in *Doctor Who*, and Manchester United were fronted by Lou Macari. (It's okay, I'm English. It makes sense to me.) It was a golden age, a gilded era, and it's been downhill all the way since then.

Today? Well, if I were twelve today, maybe I'd be just as happy. Some new painted fairy is Ziggy Stardust, Katy Manning is making *Doctor Who* spin-off audios, and Manchester United have Lou Macari in the commentary box when they play. It's still a golden age, a gilded era, and we remain happily poised at the very top of the slope, with the downhill crash still to come. And, if that's the case, then we're okay. Classic rock is not dead. There's no need to fear the Reaper. The music that we know and love is alive and well and throbbing from an iPod near you.

And if you believe that, then you're even stupider than the music industry thinks you are.

CHAPTER ONE

Lenny Kravitz for President, or, Piss Off, Sonny, and Take Your Vapid Whining with You

In which we refamiliarize ourselves with the music of a distant age and realize that the reason we still enjoy it is, everything since then has been rubbish.

CLASSIC ROCK IS MUSIC WITHOUT FRONTIERS. It is music that was created within the most unfettered of environments, devoid of any expectation or notion beyond creating a great record. Just as Beethoven, Bach, and Brahms never sat down and said, "I think I'll write some classical music today," so neither Ted Nugent nor Nazareth ever woke up and thought, "I'll write a classic rock song today." But they accomplished it anyway, because they understood the first cardinal law of rock 'n' roll:

Be true to yourself.

To have one's music branded classic rock is a privilage, not a right, to be earned via one of the hardest roads that any song could

Born to Be Wild Was Born to Be Covered: Ten Essential Revisits

Mars Bonfire—from the LP *Faster Than the Speed of Life* (1969). The composer's original, and what an odd beast it is, a soft-rocking semi-country anthem, and so politely annotated that even the line about "heavy metal thunder" sounds like he's asking you to pass the *petits pois*.

Jim Dandy—from the LP *The Art of the Motorcycle* (2005). Go, Jim Dandy, go!

Duane Allman—from the LP *Anthology 2* (1974). Jazzier than it ought to be, but Duane's drawl sounds suitably debauched, and the rhythm percolates like a heart attack.

Ace Kefford—from the LP *Ace the Face* (2004). Arthur Brown and Dolly the Sheep had a baby, and they called it former Move man Kefford's lead vocal.

Kim Fowley—from the LP *Born to Be Wild* (1969). Arch-prankster Fowley is as Fowley does. A horns-and-organ-led instrumental, cheesy as a summer breeze, breezy as a block of Brie.

The Cult—from the LP *Electric* (1987). Ian Astbury and the Cult had already recorded the song so many times in theory that they really didn't need to do it for real. But they did . . . and it sounds a lot like the Blue Öyster Cult. Only slower.

Blue Öyster Cult—single version (1975). A wholesale revision splices on an Apache war drums guitar riff, as the BÖC transplant the wastes of Altamont to the streets of Dodge City, and all the Hells Angels ride in on horseback. There's also a live version on the flip of the 45, a Mach 10 demolition that you at least ought to hear.

Ozzy Osbourne—from the LP *Prince of Darkness* (2005). A duet with Miss Piggy the Muppet. You can see he really took it seriously.

Status Quo—from the LP *Riffs* (2005). Britain's longest-running barroom boogie band grab hold of rock's most sainted anthem and make it sound just like every other record they've ever made. As all of Quo's best records should do.

Slade—from the LP *Slade Alive* (1971). Pure mayhem, with Noddy Holder howling the odds, and Dave Hill's guitar locked and leering.

travel. It is not enough to have gained the love of your listeners and the respect of your peers. Pearl Jam achieved both of those goals long ago. But admiration alone is like water down the drain if your music is a featureless, charmless drone, and longevity is the price we pay for not encouraging a band to break up sooner.

A classic rock classic needs substance and soul before it can attain that standing. It could be a bluesy belter, a progressive charmer, a metal monster, a hard rock cruncher. It can be anything it wants to be. But, from the instant the first downstroke ricochets into earshot, to the second when the final notes echo off your brainpan, the song must stand not only as a magic carpet ride for the listener's soul, but also as a sonic record of a singular moment, firmly cemented in time and place. Play Pearl Jam's first album today and all it will remind you of is the last migraine you had. Play their latest and you will be asleep before the first song has stopped sounding like cold Hot Tuna.

There was a "golden age" of classic rock, a decadelong span that stretches from the first glorious flourishes of FM rock radio in the late 1960s to a point somewhere around the mid- to late 1970s.

But, from "Born to Be Wild" to "The Boys Are Back in Town," from the searing blues of Free to the operatic bombast of Meatloaf, classic rock is not about dates or time frames or history. It is about snatching the listener out of the humdrum here-and-now, and taking off . . . heading out on the highway, looking for adventure, and climbing so high. . . .

Which is precisely what we did.

The audience at which classic rock was aimed was the wave of baby boomers who hit high school and college in time for the '70s. Born a little earlier, they'd have been wetting their panties for the Dave Clark Five. A little later, and they would have been raining phlegm down on the Clash. Later still, they'd have been treated to such distinguished delights as Mr. Mister and Simply Red.

But demographics have nothing to do with the reasons why the music still resonates. Classic rock in its purest guise might be indelibly looped into a specific passage of time, but the power of the music reaches infinitely beyond that, to create a timeless bubble in which all men are equal, all albums are exciting, and all riffs rock your socks off. You listen and you are filled with a freewheeling sense of absolute invincibility. You concentrate and you want to play air guitar.

Deathless moments of endorphin-pumping pleasure abound. That moment in *The Song Remains the Same*, where Jimmy Page, playing "Stairway to Heaven," unleashes the most strident solo of his life, and that despite being weighted down by that most extravagantly preposterous of all period accoutrements, the double-necked guitar.

The drum solo and scream that reignite "Won't Get Fooled Again," once the keyboard passage has run its course. The pregnant pause as Springsteen counts the band back in for the final verse of "Born to Run." And the tiny break in David Bowie's "Young Americans" when he proves that he, too, knows what we're talking about, and demands, "Ain't there one damn song that can make me . . . break down and cry?"

That's it! Records that hit you on so many levels, so many fronts, that your skin prickles, your hair tingles, your eyes fill with water, *and there's not a goddamn thing you can do about it.* Tramps like us, baby! Down at Dino's bar and grill. If I leave here tomorrow. . . .

Time and place are irrelevant. So are musical labels. All that matters is that the moment hits you hard, and classic rock does it. By comparison, the only money shot that matters in modern music, by which we mean just about every rock record made since 1976 (and certainly every one since 1980), is the sound of the cash register clattering. You want to know the *real* difference between the Foo Fighters and Focus? About $30 million.

Steaming out of the sound track to *Easy Rider* (and no, they don't make movies like that anymore, either), Steppenwolf's version of (the magnificently named) Mars Bonfire's "Born to Be Wild" may or may not have been the first classic rock hit. Seven or so years later, Boston's "More Than a Feeling" was probably the last. But, again, such accolades are meaningful only if you want to play fascist with chronology. Having already delineated the classic rock era, we will now disassemble it.

Any number of Beatles numbers, from the existentialist undercurrents of "Help!" through the backwards guitar psychedelia of "Tomorrow Never Knows," bristle with both the intellectual and the impulsive energies that define a classic rock song. So does Dylan's entire *Highway 61 Revisited* cycle, as it builds toward the savage entertainments of "Desolation Row."

At the other end of the timescale, Meatloaf's *Bat Out of Hell* was so deliciously extravagant and geared for grandiosity that you can quite forgive the Loaf for thus inspiring any number of subsequent heavy metal squawkers. Likewise, the Kinks emerged from a decade-old chrysalis as occasionally overachieving English eccentrics to people the late '70s and early '80s with a string of solidly excellent albums, plus the last essential double live album of the age.

Perhaps the most vibrant influence on what became classic rock, however, was Donovan, all the more so since he seems among the most unlikely. Beloved though this tousle-haired ragamuffin remains, his reputation today is still so bound up in the winsome hippie-dippiness of his later '60s work that even oldies radio only sniffs around a handful of songs, not one of which is "Atlantis."

But "Season of the Witch," a track from 1966's *Sunshine Superman* album, not only helped dictate the musical paths that the still-formative psychedelia would take, it has also become the subject of some staggeringly adventurous covers, themselves emblematic of all the energies that what we now call classic rock would demand.

Powerful enough for the song to transcend any performer, period renditions by Vanilla Fudge, Pesky Gee (forerunners of Britain's legendary Black Widow), Al Kooper, Mike Bloomfield, and the jazz-rock fusion of the Julie Driscoll/Brian Auger Trinity all toyed with the song's potential for elongated experimentation.

Richard Thompson, Stephen Stills, and Dr. John have each brought their unique energies to bear on the song, and while Cindy Lee Berryhill and Tom Constanten, who have done more recent takes of "Season," may or may not labor under the conceit that they are contributing something "new" to the song, their performances are two more toward an eclectic number that even "Born to Be Wild" cannot claim. When FM radio first crackled to life, "Season of the Witch" was as much an airplay staple as any of rock's harder-hitting contenders.

A quick reminder for readers who still think FM was just a turgid late '70s movie with music by the interminably dreary Steely Dan.

From the moment it appeared in the almost-late 1960s, FM radio was dedicated to album rock; that is, to those then-emergent bands that believed that their statements were entirely bound up within the breadth of an entire LP, and who barely gave a hoot about what had previously been the hard currency of the music industry, the seven-inch 45.

Ever since Dylan devoted one full side of his 1966 *Blonde on Blonde* double album to a single song, the driftingly beautiful "Sad Eyed Lady of the Lowlands," the notion of following suit had haunted rock's most pioneering souls.

The previously accepted parameters of a single rock song (three minutes—verse chorus verse, middle eight, fade) had already been shattered when the Animals' "House of the Rising Sun" ran on for almost five minutes in 1964 and did away with the chorus altogether. Dylan topped that with "Like a Rolling Stone" the following year; the Rolling Stones crowned that with eleven minutes of "Going Home," a highlight of their *Aftermath* album. The Mothers of Invention went even further with "The Return of the Son of Monster Magnet," and emerged with twelve minutes of percussion and shouting that may not have made it onto AM radio too often, but neither did "Going Home."

FM rewarded them accordingly. No less than the musicians who rode the late 1960s into fresh fields of expression, American disc jockeys were expanding the frontiers of what they could get away with, leaping aboard the FM wave bands with some of the most courageous programming of all time. Once, it was considered revolutionary to play two singles back-to-back without a break for chatter or commercials. Now, entire sides of albums were being aired without interruption, or songs that were the length of an album side, with the chitchat kept to a mumbled acknowledgment of one sponsor or another, dropped in between two vast sprawling chunks of rock.

It wasn't all exemplary, of course. For every "Sad Eyed Lady of the Lowlands," there was an "Under the Mersey Wall," a side-long experiment in bleeps and burps that consumed half of Beatle George's second solo album. For every "Spoonful" that Cream stretched to superhuman lengths, there was a "Toad," and it seems incredible today that radio would ever devote sixteen minutes of airtime to a drum solo.

But the actual quality of an epic was always going to be secondary to the fact it *was* an epic, because an enterprising DJ could get an awful lot done in the time it took to play through. He could roll a joint (on a gatefold LP cover—one reason why very few Grateful Dead fans ever replaced their vinyl with CD) and smoke the best bit. He could go to the bathroom or deflower a maiden (yes, DJs got groupies too. Incredible, isn't it?). He could even phone his girlfriend and eat his dinner and, if he hadn't quite finished when the song was over: "That was so cool, let's hear the other side."

Listeners felt the same way as well. Or maybe they were too stoned to turn the radio off. Either way, by the end of the decade, FM ruled the airwaves, and rock, in all its fast-emergent guises, ruled FM.

Vanilla Fudge's Quaalude-paced plod through the Supremes' "You Keep Me Hanging On" spun out of FM to become a major hit single. The Doors' Oedipal epic "The End" left late-night listeners spellbound at the thought of what Jimbo wanted to do to his mother. Pink Floyd's "Interstellar Overdrive" and "Saucerful of Secrets" examined the furthest reaches of outer space by transporting you to the darkest depths of its innermost counterpart.

Like Life, Side Two
Is a Long Song: 1970–1975

Humble Pie (LP *Rocking the Fillmore*)—"Walk on Gilded Splinters" (1970)

ELP (LP *Tarkus*)—"Tarkus" (1971)

Jethro Tull (LP *Thick as a Brick*)—"Thick as a Brick" (1972)

Genesis (LP *Foxtrot*)—"Supper's Ready" (1972)

Caravan (LP *In the Land of Grey and Pink*)—"Nine Feet Underground" (1971)

Yes (LP *Close to the Edge*)—"Close to the Edge" (1972)

Neil Young (LP *Journey Through the Past*)—"Words" (1972)

Focus (LP *Focus III*)—"Answers? Questions! Questions? Answers!" (1972)

Kraftwerk (LP *Autobahn*)—"Autobahn" (1975)

Pink Floyd (LP *Meddle*)—"Echoes" (1971)

True, you could count on the fingers of Django Reinhardt's left hand the number of radio stations that aired the Velvet Underground's "Sister Ray," seventeen minutes of feedback, noise, and Lou Reed happily having his ding-dong sucked. But Quicksilver Messenger Service's "The Fool" felt almost as good, while Iron Butterfly's "In A Gadda Da Vida" went for on so long that you could pop out to do the shopping and it would still be churning when you returned. By 1969, even the Beatles could not resist bleeding nine of the eleven songs on side two of *Abbey Road* into one long suite, and leaving the DJs to sort out what to do with the odd couple.

And where the '60s left off, the '70s had to continue.

Of course, not everybody likes a side-long song; or, more accurately, not everybody appreciates them. As a schoolboy around 1973 or so, just discovering prog rock, I was torn between two Van der Graaf Generator albums, while knowing I could afford only one.

Aerosol Grey Machine (nine tracks)? Or *Pawn Hearts* (three)? I was young, I was callow, I wanted value for money! I went for the former, even after the guy behind the counter (yes, him again) warned me that it wasn't very good.

A week later I was back again and, bless his heart, he let me exchange it. I still play *Pawn Hearts* at least once a month today. And why? Because the side-long "Plague of Lighthouse Keepers" remains one of the most turbulent, traumatic, and constantly surprising pieces of music ever consigned to vinyl.

From one extreme to another. With their eyes firmly on the extended epic, Van der Graaf Generator released a mere handful of singles and didn't particularly care if anybody bought them. Most of the other "album bands" of the day behaved likewise. Singles were for kids, man, singles were for suckers. Overnight, the musical genre that author Nik Cohn so exquisitely tagged "superpop," in which every band that was worth its salt did its fighting in the singles chart, was over. Never again would you switch on the radio and hear, in one glorious burst, the Beatles' "Eleanor Rigby," the Who's "I'm a Boy," the Small Faces' "All or Nothing," the Stones' "Have You Seen Your Mother," and the Beach Boys' "God Only Knows," all battling it out for supremacy on the same week's pop chart.

Instead, singles were things that slipped out of new albums, preferably when no-one was looking, and when the newly bearded and sunglassed artists were quizzed upon how seriously they took their jobs, the fact that they weren't into 45s was usually the make-or-break point. They meant it as well.

But was the 45 dead? Like hell it was. Regardless of what the bands intended, the record companies continued issuing the little darlings, because old habits died hard, and when they crossed over into the pop charts, all manner of magic was possible. "Born to Be Wild" roared its way to number two on the *Billboard* chart, an achievement that was not quite an unprecedented success, but was nevertheless a shocker for anybody who believed that rock was rock, and pop was for the kiddies. And, as the '60s moved into the '70s, that

17

song kicked open the door through which a host of other album-rockers, FM mainstays, would march.

Even the most stubbornly standoffish bands wound up with hit singles despite themselves. Renowned hairies Black Sabbath, Deep Purple, Yes, Curved Air, Argent, Genesis, and Pink Floyd scored sizable smashes on one side or other of the Atlantic, without ever taking their eyes off the LP-shaped ball. It is also true that, while both Led Zeppelin and Emerson, Lake & Palmer made a serious show of never releasing 45s in their British homeland, they were considerably less squeamish in America.

ELP's "Lucky Man" and "From the Beginning" both made the Top 50, while Led Zeppelin simply clocked up the biggies—the Top 5 "Whole Lotta Love," the Top 20 "Immigrant Song," "Black Dog," and "D'Yer Maker." Had they only figured out a way of cramming all eight minutes of "Stairway to Heaven" into three minutes' worth of 45-rpm vinyl without having to take a pair of scissors to it, they would certainly have soared even higher.

FM marched on. The '60s bled out of the hourglass, and snatched away a few old favorites. But the new decade quickly replaced them with bands whose names still resonate today.

The Blue Öyster Cult were American psychos who emerged fully formed and full-blooded on a wave of scintillating imagery. They swept from the sleek majesty of wartime German jet planes to a litany of leather-whipped sexual fantasies, and topped it off with a virtual alphabet's worth of arcane symbols and secret mythologies. Sunglassed and surly, the Cult kicked their first album off with a biker anthem ("Transmaniacon MC") that made "Born to Be Wild" sound like a bicycle ride—and then they transformed "Born to Be Wild" as well. Plus, they insisted they knew Lucifer so well that they called him by his first name. "Hey, Lou!" Of course they went down the pan in the end, abandoning the abandon in favor of a smearless streak of soundalike soft rockers, but for the few years when they mattered, they *really* mattered.

Ten Hit Singles by Bands Who Don't Do Singles, Man

Led Zeppelin—"Whole Lotta Love" (#4, USA, 1970)

Black Sabbath—"Paranoid" (#4, UK, 1970)

ELP—"From the Beginning" (#39, USA, 1971)

Deep Purple—"Black Night" (#2, UK, 1970)

Yes—"Roundabout" (#13, USA, 1972)

Curved Air—"Back Street Luv" (#4, UK, 1971)

Argent—"Hold Your Head Up" (#5, USA/UK, 1972)

Hawkwind—"Silver Machine" (#2, UK, 1972)

Pink Floyd—"Money" (#13, US, 1973)

Genesis (while they were still good)—"I Know What I Like" (#18, UK, 1974)

Free were a teenage British blues band whose "All Right Now" rode a riff that rewrote the rock guitar lexicon, but whose greatest achievements were bound up in the preternatural interplay between vocalist Paul Rodgers and guitarist Paul Kossoff.

The Guess Who. They may have looked like a badly dressed haberdashers' convention, but Steppenwolf's Canadian countrymen not only extolled the evils of an "American Woman," they genuinely sounded like they meant it.

The Latin rhythms of Santana seethed and broiled around a lifelong Cinco de Mayo. There was the twin-axe majesty of Wishbone Ash; the space rock operatics of Hawkwind; the jangling keys of Supertramp; the crunching riffs of the Groundhogs; the serene sonic fountains of Gentle Giant; the snarling nastiness of Bloodrock. . . .

Indeed, it was remarkable just how all-encompassing the prevalent tastes of the day could be. We are so accustomed today to having our broadcast music served up to us in delicately proportioned bite-size slices of homogeny that, after just a few hours of exposure to the mundane silliness of the average radio station, it's easy to forget (and perhaps painful to remember) a time when radio programmers did not arrange their wares like books on a shelf and boast a Beatles half hour every evening at drive time.

It was a time when a flick of a switch could send your ears spinning from the flute-and-warble weirdness of Jethro Tull to the southern-fried boogie of Lynyrd Skynyrd, from the West Coast groove of the Doobie Brothers to the metallic crash of Grand Funk Railroad.

It was an era when—ah, but you are probably tired of being told how good the good old days were. You know that already. What you are far more curious about is, when did they end? Why did they change? How did we end up *here* when we ought to be *there*?

Well, it's a long and very convoluted story, and there are certainly places where you might well scratch your head and wonder, What the devil is this idiot on about? You might not *want* to listen to Captain Beefheart's *Trout Mask Replica* on eight-track, or buy a denim jacket simply so you can embroider a Black Sabbath logo onto the back. You might disagree entirely that three minutes spent with Gary Glitter's "Rock and Roll" (Parts One, Two, and, subsequently, Three through Six—take your pick) are worth a lifetime listening to Amy Winehouse (and how cripplingly apt a name is that? Jesus, it's not even worth making a joke about it). You might even like Radiohead and genuinely believe that *OK Computer* is the most meaningful modern rock album ever made.

But I'm glad you added "modern" to that sentence. Because that's precisely the point. It's rock, but it's *modern*. Which is akin to waking up one morning to find a scorpion inside your most comfortable sock. Sitting down to your favorite meal and discovering that every course has brussels sprouts in it, and that includes the wine.

Back when you were at school, and the teacher was blithering on about Boston Tea Parties and the GNP of the USSR, you were transcribing the words to "Volunteers" in your head and mourning the fate of John Sinclair, "in the stir for breathing air."

Or after class, on the playground. Who taught you more about the opposite sex? King Crimson's "Ladies of the Road" and whispered rumors of a Stones song called "Cocksucker Blues"? Or Mrs. Wossername's biology class, where you dissected a frog's reproductive system?

And so on. Music makes you, music shapes you—music even determines the kind of person you will grow up to be. Which in the '60s and '70s was fine. You're a Deadhead, I'm a Deadhead, let's go off and smoke some Moby Grape LPs together. But today? Can you even imagine what the present generation is going to turn into?

And would you even want to?

CHAPTER TWO

Selling Postcards of the Hanging, or, This Is the End, Distended Friend

In which the convoluted history of classic rock is spread out on the banquet table, and we feast on the music that we know we'll love forever.

IN 1968, THE MUSIC INDUSTRY was changed forever. It was the first year in which album sales outstripped singles sales in America, by 192 million to 187 million, and though that was not necessarily a surprise, it certainly opened a few eyes.

A quick recap: For two or three years now, as bands grew more confident and ambitious, the LP had developed further and further away from its original function as a repository for a handful of singles, their attendant B-sides, and a bunch of filler that they knocked out as an afterthought.

Bob Dylan's *Bringing It All Back Home*, in spring 1965, commenced the progression. One side acoustic folkiness, the other side driving rock, it was Dylan's transition from Jesus to Judas laid out for all to see, and it became his first Top 10 American hit. By the time he followed through with *Highway 61 Revisited*, later that same year, the Beatles were about to release *Rubber Soul*, their own first distinctly *driven* collection; and, when the following year brought Dylan's *Blonde on Blonde*, the Stones' *Aftermath*, and the Beatles' *Revolver*, all seemingly within nanoseconds of one another, the die was cast.

By the end of 1966, San Francisco's Grateful Dead and Jefferson Airplane, L.A.'s Mothers of Invention and New York's Velvet Underground had all signed major record deals without any expectation whatsoever of scoring (or even seriously releasing) hit singles; through 1967, the likes of Quicksilver Messenger Service, the Steve Miller Band, and Creedence Clearwater Revival had the same feverish gleam in their eyes. For each of them, their music, like their audience, was geared toward the long-playing disc.

Nobody told any of them to make that switch. They just made it, all stricken by the instinctive understanding that rock music had gone as far as it could in one direction. It was time to start moving in another.

Nineteen sixty-eight was the year that rock grew up, and its audience grew with it. Not into adulthood, with all the graying, bearded maturity which that condition normally portends, but into a state of calm, reasoning responsibility, and the awareness that, if governments were no longer capable of leading, then somebody else needed to step up to the plate and do it for them.

A bunch of hairy musicians, most of them scarcely five years out of high school, and a lot of them addled by the pharmaceutical delights that washed like rain through the culture of the day, were nobody's dream leaders. Neither, though the music they made was rarely less than serious, were there necessarily any true-life lessons to be drawn from "The Ballad of You and Me and Pooneil" (Jefferson

Airplane), "Texas Radio and the Big Beat" (the Doors), or "Voodoo Chile" (Hendrix).

But still, by 1968, the façade of love and peace that had sustained youth fashion through the summer of 1967 had finally been punctured. The three-year-old Vietnam War was turning ever uglier every day, with the previous year's death toll of 9,353 Americans more than double that of the first two years combined. The ferocity of the New Year's Tet Offensive suggested that, this year, the numbers would be climbing even higher.

Moods had changed. Flower power blossomed for a while, but the edifice crumbled quickly. By the end of the year, the peace-and-loveniks who'd been born with such high hopes were largely lying crushed and despondent beneath the weight of their own Utopian expectations. Culturally, the backlash was apocalyptic. Musically, it was even more brutal.

In 1967, the Beatles were singing of meter maids, Mr. Kite, and meetings with men from the motor trade. In 1968, they were focusing on blistered fingers, warm guns, and weeping guitars. In 1967, the Rolling Stones were talking of lanterns and rainbows and singing it all together. In 1968, they were scorching the earth with "Jumping Jack Flash," and nailing jailbait with stray cat blues. In 1967, the Who dreamed of Heinz Baked Beans and cities in the sky. In 1968 they were foisting a new messiah upon us.

The antiwar movement was gaining vivid momentum; the civil rights movement was gathering arms. Again the previous year, race riots had become commonplace throughout America's inner cities, but now the rioters were formidably organized, as Dr. Martin Luther King's dream of peaceful black equality was translated into the gun-toting Black Panthers' cry of Black Power. In February 1968, in Brooklyn's Bedford-Stuyvesant, eighth-grade students all but rioted in protest of the quality of school lunches; in March, Columbia University was stricken by a daylong boycott of classes, in protest over the war. At the University of Wisconsin in Madison, antiwar protesters

planted four hundred white crosses on the lawn outside the adminis-
trative buildings, beneath a notice that proclaimed them "the class of
1968."

The establishment responded in kind. The police started fighting
back. In Los Angeles, the sheriff's office contemplated the purchase of
a fleet of armored cars, all the better with which to pin those weari-
some flower children up against the wall. In Detroit, they purchased
an army-surplus half-track, solely to keep the citizenry in order. In
Prague, the Soviets sent the tanks in; in Paris, the scent of marijuana
was choked beneath the stench of tear gas. And from the depths of
the bunkers where the nuclear arsenals flower, *The Bulletin of Atomic
Scientists* prepared for Armageddon by pushing forward one hand on
the Doomsday Clock, their own iconic contribution to the shaky state
of the world. For more than four years, ever since the missile crisis
days that drove Dylan to warn of Hard Rain, the clock's hands had
been frozen at twelve minutes to midnight. Now they hovered five
minutes closer.

Hippie became a dirty word; *student, pacifist,* and *protester* likewise. Visiting California in 1967, English tourists Cream expressed
their astonishment at the freedom that seemed to permeate the very
streets of the inner cities. True, not every passing cop was willing to
look the other way when he stumbled on a gang of kids taking a
crafty toke, but he wasn't about to start cracking skulls with his night-
stick, either. Now, a passerby only needed to look like he needed a
haircut to be hauled down to the station, and maybe dragged along to
the induction center too.

The temperature continued rising. At least two concerts on
Cream's spring tour of the United States were canceled outright as
university authorities clamped down on anything that might provoke
any kind of unrest. Naturally, rock 'n' roll music was universally
regarded among the most potent flash points of all. Equally naturally,
it rose to the challenge with a vengeance.

Where the music led, the media followed.

For anybody brought up on the gossip-clad music press of the 1980s and beyond, who knows the media only as the toothless mouthpiece of whichever conglomerate is buying this week's round of drinks, it is difficult to imagine a time when the press wasn't merely "opinionated" (as in, "This label gave us more freebies than that one, so we'll be extra nice to their acts this week") but also massively influential; when it wasn't simply capable of making or breaking a band (ditto) but found an intellectual joy in exercising that capability.

That era lasted little more than a decade. The *International Times*—a London underground paper that launched in October 1966 through the largesse of Paul McCartney (among others) to document the local scene through the inspired writings of Mick Farren, Barry Miles, Germaine Greer, and Bill Levy, among others—started it.

America's own *IT*, the San Francisco—based *Rolling Stone*, followed a year later, aping the Londoners' recipe of hard-hitting cultural criticism and observation via its own well-chosen network of correspondents. Every music magazine that sprang to prominence in the years that followed modeled itself on one or the other of these.

Ah, but independent spirit and thought were never going to pay all the bills. By the end of the 1970s, only the most obscure backroom fanzine could claim to be completely free of any outside influence (and that was only because nobody knew it existed). The free press was a thing of the past.

But while it flourished, it could be ruthless, with even the most flippant assessments capable of seriously impacting upon an artist's ego.

When *Rolling Stone*'s Jon Landau condemned Cream for being so stultifyingly complacent in 1968, Eric Clapton came close to quitting the band. When the British press nailed Jethro Tull in the mid-70s, Ian Anderson contemplated retiring altogether. Suddenly and, seemingly without warning, musicians were being held accountable for more than their ability to string together a catchy chorus. Every aspect of their performance, from their musical prowess to their literary influences, from their improvisational abilities to their instrumental eclecticism, and on to their dress sense and political convictions, was now open for criticism.

It was not a harsh environment, at least at first. It was a nurturing one. "Don't be lazy," the critics appeared to be chiding. "Don't be scared. There's a whole world of expression out there, just waiting to be explored. So explore it!" Even Landau's Cream crucifixion merely suggested that the band *could* be on a collision course with irrelevance, not that they had already crashed into it. It was a warning, not a news flash. It proved that people *cared*.

"It was a marvelous time, and it really was incredibly exciting," Deep Purple organist Jon Lord reflected. "It was a wonderful time to be a musician, because there were no rules and there were a whole number of different bands making new kinds of music. That was a very special time for musical creativity."

Recalling Cream's first visit to the Fillmore West in 1967, Eric Clapton confessed the trio was initially shocked, and rapidly mortified, to discover that scarcely anybody was dancing to their music, and hardly more were even applauding. It was only as the evening wore on that they realized the audience weren't sitting there hating them. They were *listening*, and Clapton described the night as the first time "I experienced the kind of more introverted or serious or introspective attitude toward our music, which seemed to go hand in hand with hallucinogenic drugs, or grass, or whatever. It was more into a 'head' thing."

Now the "head" thing was everywhere, and others were quick to follow Cream's example. This was not necessarily a good thing. You may think that everything in the classic rock garden was perfect, but I'm here to tell you that it wasn't. Clapton, Bruce, and Baker built their reputation upon extended jam sessions and virtuoso solos. Now, every group that had a set to fill, but only enough songs for half of it, was scrambling to show that they were great players too, and unleashing so many solos that an entire generation of gig-goers never knew how it felt to stand and watch an entire concert uninterrupted. There was always one excuse or another to hit the bar or, and it usually began with the words, "Our sax player has a little number he'd like to play for you now, and it's called . . . ."

Although Ginger Baker was the first rock drummer to consign a solo to wax, when he unleashed the tiresome "Toad," it was Led Zeppelin's John Bonham who truly ignited that particular fashion. From the moment "Moby Dick" surfaced in 1969, expanding out of *Led Zeppelin II* to consume fifteen, sometimes twenty, minutes of the stage show, drummers who had not even grasped the basic elements of rhythm were suddenly miking up more drums than they could ever possibly reach, and walloping everything in sight.

It was a grotesque development and, according to Zeppelin manager Peter Grant, Bonzo himself resented it furiously. When he went to a live show, he wanted to be entertained and impressed. Most of the solos he found himself sitting through would have been laughed out of Zeppelin's rehearsal room.

He never apologized for unleashing the plague in the first place, though. Why should he? Did Picasso say sorry every time another bad painter daubed his doodles on canvas? Does Peter O'Toole cringe whenever he sits through another Tom Hanks movie? Can Janis Joplin really be blamed for every squawking harridan who has followed in her footsteps? There is good and bad in every endeavor, and Bonham was lucky enough that, because he was so good, he did not have to take responsibility for all the bad he inspired.

Viewed dispassionately from several decades hence, it is painfully obvious that a lot more dross was unleashed by sundry grandstanding bandstanders than decent (or even listenable) music, and that few of the solos scorching ears at the turn of the 1960s actually bear listening to today. Even Martin Barre who, with Jethro Tull, was responsible for some awfully protracted one-man routines, confessed in 1997, "I suppose all that early emphasis on solos was a hangover from the jazz era, where everybody had their solos. In some ways, it reflects on

Ten Classic Rock Album Tracks That You've Never Played More Than Once (Probably)

Led Zeppelin—"Moby Dick" (drum solo)

Deep Purple—"The Mule" (drum solo)

Cream—"Toad" (drum solo)

Grand Funk—"TNUC" (drum solo)

Santana—Soul Sacrifice (drum solo)

Grateful Dead—"Drums" (dunno, haven't heard it)

Rush—"Rhythm Method" (drum solo)

Led Zeppelin—Bonzo's Montreux (drum solo)

Yes—"Heart of the Sunrise" (live drum solo)

Phil Collins—"I Missed Again" (drummer solo)

how boring the music was." But, he added, "We got away with it." Cue fiendish Faustian cackle and a puff of diabolical smoke.

However, protracted solos were merely the icing on the new musical cake for musicians who dared to venture into the unknown. With the freedom to play *what* you liked, there came the freedom to sound *how* you liked, pleasures that might seem alien today, when every new band seems to have its parameters outlined in the first contract they sign ("Your name is the Walkmen, and you will sound like a shitty cassette blaring through some cheap foam headphones"), but which were crucial to the development of classic rock.

Some groups bunched themselves together, and assaulted the unknown en masse:

Acid rock was a blanket term that could accommodate any band whose music seemed to play off (or play into) the effects that a tab of decent LSD could induce, with the corollary, applied to the worst records of the day, being a comparison to a really bad trip. A tie-dye T-shirt was the only uniform you needed; add a guitar solo the length of Broadway, and you were off.

Jefferson Airplane, the Grateful Dead, Quicksilver, Moby Grape, Hot Tuna—the San Francisco sound of the late 1960s was built upon the premise of acid rock, and it glowed like a million stars. Twenty-some years later, an entire new generation of groups would emerge to take these same time-honored touchstones as the root of their own music. But the jam band revolution was never going to succeed for one simple reason: The original acid rockers took acid. This new crop would probably set their lawyers on you if you even asked if they knew what it was.

Southern rock placed a geographic spin on things, with the insistence that any band hailing from beneath the Mason-Dixon Line was somehow genetically predisposed to merge mile-long guitar passages with a drawling twang and a bottle of Jack Daniels. The Allman Brothers, Lynyrd Skynyrd, the Marshall Tucker Band, and the Dixie Dregs mixed metaphors like Madonna mixes accents ("Today I'm frightfully English, but tomorrow I'll be an Ah-meh-ri-caaaaaaaaaan"). The jam bands tapped into this time warp too—but again, they got it wrong. When Duane Allman nailed a solo, it stayed nailed. When Phish laid one down, it was sneaking out the back way before they'd even thought of a title for it.

Satanic rock came scything out of the psychedelic underground as the successor (logical or otherwise) to the Beatles' drive into Transcendental Meditation, picking up on Hollywood's long-running obsession with horror epics by posing one simple question:

If people were willing to pay good money to be scared by a movie, how much would they pay to be scared by a rock band? Black Sabbath led the charge, even if Ozzy Osbourne did later admit that the closest they ever got to black magic was the Cadbury confection of the same name; but Black Widow and Coven mined the same musical mindset with proselytizing conviction, and Jimmy Page famously lived in a house that once belonged to Aleister Crowley.

In years to come, acts like Danzig, Rigor Mortis, and a host of (oddly) Scandinavian metal bands would skip through similarly Satanic pastures and arouse a lot of ill feeling from a lot of very noble Christian onlookers. Unfortunately, they missed out on the most basic equation of all. When people say the devil has all the best tunes, they mean it. Forty minutes of directionless thrashing while the singer removes his larynx with a chain saw will not set Beelzebub's toes a-tapping.

California rose up with a **West Coast** sound that added some country licks to the singer-songwriter fare that had been making such an indolent nuisance of itself since Leonard Cohen slashed his first figurative wrist, and induced some dynamic recordings from Linda Ronstadt and Jackson Browne, while inspiring the Doobie Brothers (who weren't brothers) to create some of the finest melodic rock (which wasn't rock) of the day.

The Doobies are best remembered today for the multiple harmonies of "Black Water," "China Grove," and "Long Train Running," and some magnificent photographs of the band on stage, all but lost within the clouds of dry ice that billowed around them. But that's a damned fine memorial when you think about it, and it's still an awful lot better advertisement for Cal-i-for-nee-ay than the self-aggrandizing nonsense that today considers itself emblematic of the state. Let me just mention the Red Hot Chili Peppers. You know what I mean.

So much for the genres that arose in the golden age. Equally important, and maybe more so, were those bands that never really nailed allegiance to any particular flag, who just went out there and played.

And played and played and played.

Looking exactly like the grouchy biker who hangs out by the Stop & Shop, Bob Seger came rumbling out of Detroit with his Silver Bullet Band and a live set that is now wall-to-wall classic rock memories.

1976's "Night Moves" is the one that everybody gets stuck on today, a sprawling epic of adolescent sexuality and energy that picked up on the same mood that *American Graffiti* set in motion in the movies, to portray the past as a foreign country where life was actually fun again. But you could track back through a recording career that was almost a decade old at that point, and never come up with a song you hadn't fallen in love to at least once.

In America, Status Quo are remembered only for a lightweight psych hit in 1968, the twee twiddles of "Pictures of Matchstick Men." Elsewhere around the planet, though, they're Brobdingnagian, a balls-out blues boogie bar band that you could call the UK's answer to ZZ Top, but you would need a serious slapping if you did. True, they've taken more missteps than a one-legged opportunist rock divorcée on *Celebrity Come Dancing*, but they've remained Quo through it all, and "Down the Dustpipe," "Caroline," "Down Down," and more (so many more) will still make you shimmy like your sister Sue.

Wishbone Ash, too, found the United States a hard nut to crack, and that despite cutting one album, 1971's *Argus*, that races second only to Zeppelin (and the best of Zeppelin at that) when it comes to combining hard rock, melody, and English folk influences into one coherent whole. There's nothing as deliciously crafted as "Stairway to Heaven," or as chillingly intense as "Since I've Been Loving You." They never rock 'n' roll like "rock 'n' roll." But there's no room for self-indulgence or artiness either. No sprawling mistakes, no over-wrought histrionics, no quarter. Just solid songwriting, stunning musicianship, and a shroud of misty pagan beauty that eases out of the artwork to permeate the entire disc with such cohesion that, even today, sundry surviving Ashers still offer periodic re-creations of the album.

Do you remember Nazareth? Howling out of Scotland to make some of the loudest records of the age, they seriously gave Joni Mitchell fans a coronary when they turned their attentions to "This Flight Tonight." They also did a sterling number on the old psych rocker "My White Bicycle," although radio recalls Nazareth best for a sweetly melodic cover of "Love Hurts," a performance that could be personally blamed for the invention of the power ballad if Dan McCafferty hadn't spent the entire song shouting the lyrics at the top of his luxuriously leathery lungs. "Hey, Schenectady! Can you hear me at the back? Love HURTS!"

And then there was Grand Funk Railroad, who topped the American chart with a version of "The Locomotion" that could indeed have been recorded in a railroad yard, so loud and crunchingly heavy did it sound.

Broodingly hirsute, Grand Funk were already a legend when they burst onto the scene, growing out of mid-'60s hit makers Terry Knight and the Pack (Knight remained the new band's manager) on the back of what could only be described as self-perpetuating hype. Picky about where they played, but not about informing the media of their decisions, Grand Funk built a reputation as one of the most integrity-packed bands around, and one of the most prolific. New albums appeared like clockwork, one every six months or so. They toured constantly and loudly, and by the summer 1973 release of the epochal *We're An American Band*, they were unquestionably one of the biggest draws in the country.

However, as Ritchie Blackmore once pointed out, no matter how many times he toured America, and how many fans he talked to, he had yet to meet anyone who claimed to be a Grand Funk Railroad fan. On paper, Grand Funk were massive. Their albums were surefire platinum before they were even released, their singles were mega, and they were selling out the enormo-domes that most bands had only set foot in as audience members. But you *never actually met anybody who liked Grand Funk*, which, in turn, might translate to the fact that nobody *did* like them. They bought the records to recapture the live show, they went to the live show to hang out with their friends, and they hung out with their friends because they bought the same records. There's a circularity there that, to be painfully fair to Grand Funk, is by no means exclusive to the heyday of their renown.

Foghat, the J. Geils Band, Savoy Brown, the Bob Welch—era Fleetwood Mac, Ten Years After, Uriah Heep, pre—*Comes Alive* Peter Frampton, post—Peter Frampton Humble Pie—you could compile a telephone directory filled with the bands that trailed their way across the United States through the early to mid-1970s, selling out every place they laid their hats, boosting their record sales at every port of call, and leaving absolutely no lasting mark upon anybody who witnessed them perform.

But they still made wonderful music. Twenty minutes spent with Humble Pie as they slipped through their signature reimagining of Dr. John's "Walk on Gilded Splinters" are twenty minutes of joy that few other bands could ever give you. Uriah Heep's "July Morning" is one of the greatest organ workouts this side of whichever bad '70s porn movie just flicked on in your head; and Ten Years After so stole the show at Woodstock that you can reduce the entire movie down to little more than their marathon march through "I'm Going Home."

Because it was the music that mattered. The personalities behind it, the people who actually played it—they weren't exactly irrelevant, but they weren't the focus, either. You did not go to a Jo Jo Gunne gig because you liked Curly Smith. You went because you *loved* "Run Run Run." Likewise, when Slade came over and toured through the 1970s, you didn't give a damn about Noddy Holder's mirrored hat. You wanted to get down and get with it to some of stompiest, craziest, crunchiest sounds around. Bands were the vehicle that drove music into your heart. And once it got there, it was wedged in place forever.

But the age of such limitless possibilities and glorious anonymity was coming to an end, devoured not by its popularity, or even the absurdity of collecting triple live albums by bands you'd never heard of. It would be devoured from within, by the never-ending quest for musical perfection—and for the last dime in the bank.

CHAPTER THREE

The Titanic Sails at Dawn,
or,
More Than
More Than a Feeling

In which dark shadows appear across our happy vistas, and
we stumble across a body in the ballroom. Who killed
rock 'n' roll, and how many suspects should we finger-
print before we blame Colonel Mustard?

IF YOU LOOK AT THE HISTORY OF ROCK in strictly lin-
ear fashion, it is clear that music moves in five- to seven-
year cycles. We date the original rock 'n' roll era from
somewhere around 1955, and the near-simultaneous emergence of
Bill Haley and the Comets, Elvis Presley, Jerry Lee Lewis and Little
Richard, and generally agree that it was over with by the end of
the decade, as death (Buddy Holly, Eddie Cochran), jail (Chuck
Berry), or conscription (Elvis Presley) whipped its biggest lights out
of circulation.

The British Invasion (the "beat boom" in Europe) was next, hit-
ting in 1963 with the arrival of the Beatles, the Stones, the Kinks, and

so forth, and clinging on until 1966, when a new generation of musicians grew out of both the American West Coast and the heart of swinging London, for whom musical experimentation, lyrical whimsy, and chemical inspiration combined to create psychedelia. This spent long enough morphing into prog, metal, and so forth that, by 1972, it was time for things to change again, and the UK was swept by the glam rock that heaved David Bowie, Roxy Music, the Sweet, and T. Rex to the rest of the planet. Long before anything actually happened, then, it was odds-on that 1977 or so would see music changing trains again, and so it did.

History likes to say that it was punk rock that made the difference, demolishing the concepts and conceits of old and replacing them with a new urgency and democracy. History is wrong. True, punk did shake things up a little, and it would launch a new storm of bands into the stratosphere. It also eventually morphed into new wave and alternative rock, buzzwords that saw a lot of service as the 1980s and 1990s wandered on.

But punk was essentially a *retrogression*, stripping rock away from the increasingly technical standards that were gathering speed throughout the decade so far, and driving it back to the kind of spit-and-polish basics that the early Stones, Who, and Beatles knew so well, and which every undernourished group on the club and barroom circuit had always been living with anyway. Punk was the triumph of the little people, but that's all it was. Because the big people didn't care.

Rock wasn't killed by disco, either, although a lot of Midwestern DJs seem to have built their reputations upon their propensity for launching Disco Sucks frat parties and burning great piles of Bee Gees albums. Hey, the environment thanks you for that, Brainiac.

Besides, while much of the watching rock world took solace in the sad belief that disco itself was a mere passing fad, and the whole thing would dance itself out in the end, it made some remarkable converts as it marched on through. Or, to reiterate the cry that shook half the known globe during the summer of 1978, "Ohmigod! Have you heard the new Stones single? They've gone disco!"

"Miss You," from the Stones' *Some Girls* album, is among the best songs they ever recorded, at least within their post—*Sticky Fingers* catalog. The bass is deep and throbbing, the beat is hot for teacher, and Jagger's vocals are so tightly trousered that he could have been auditioning for a walk-on part in Donna Summer's "Love to Love You Baby." But that was what disco culture was about: hedonism, humping, and not giving a damn what other people thought.

Likewise Rod Stewart's "Do Ya Think I'm Sexy?". The celebrity boyfriend of actress Britt Ekland, the cockatoo-haired one time rocker and well-known bar hopper was now seemingly dedicated to persuading Middle America to get out of its Barcaloungers for a quick, salacious grind. "If you want mah bod-eeeeee, an' ya think ah'm sex-eeeeeeeeee . . ." How many watching juveniles were scarred for life by the sight of aging parents and embarrassing uncles dry-humping the air as they pranced around to that?

"Do Ya Think I'm Sexy?" stripped away every last shred of the respectability Stewart had cultivated over the previous decade, but did he care? Not a jot. He knew, even if his detractors avoided the subject, that the song was as grandly, sweepingly raunchy as any of the misogynist anthems that he'd carved out in the past—"Every Picture Tells a Story," "Stay With Me," "Cindy Incidentally"—which, in turn, means, it was as great as them as well. Don't be fooled by the beats per minute. Rod the Mod was still a god.

So were Kiss. Nineteen seventy-nine's "I Was Made for Lovin' You" was disco enough to earn the song a spot on K-tel compilations, up there with "In the Bush" and "Boogie Oogie Oogie." And it still sounds barking mad today. But while it's true that Kiss could never, ever, be the Bee Gees, vocalist Gene Simmons turned in one mean falsetto, certainly out-squeaking the *Emotional Rescue*-era Jagger in the pseudo-castrato stakes, and does it really matter if he's off-key most of the time? It's the thought that counts, and besides, "I Was

White Dopes on Funk: Ten Great Rock Disco Songs

Kiss—"I Was Made for Loving You"

Rolling Stones—"Miss You"

Rolling Stones—"Emotional Rescue"

Rod Stewart—"Do Ya Think I'm Sexy?"

Wings—"Goodnight Tonight"

Roxy Music—"Love Is the Drug"

David Bowie—"Golden Years"

Ian Hunter—"Bastard"

Queen—"Another One Bites the Dust"

Eric Clapton—"Wonderful Tonight" (slow dance with Slowhand!)

Made for Loving You" packs one of the most salacious guitar hooks in the band's entire repertoire. Most bands would have been terrified of transforming themselves from raging metal monsters into revolving-mirror-ball minstrels over night, but not Kiss. They made even dead men dance.

The important thing is, none of this is a Bad Thing.

Yes, maybe the guilty parties should have known better.

Yes, maybe there *was* a ten-minute period when you really felt awkward about having all those Stones posters pinned to your bedroom wall, when you knew that your heroes were out at Studio Fifty-whatever, living it up with the beee-yuu-ti-ful people, and spending their earnings (which was your hard-earned cash) on another bank of strobe lights for their private Mickmobiles.

But ultimately, what difference did it make?

The rest of the Stones' album was as rocking as usual, but it wasn't *Goat's Head Soup* by a long way. Stewart was a lost cause long before he discovered those spray-on leopard-skin trousers, and Kiss hadn't made a decent record since *Rock and Roll Over*, two years earlier. Because the pendulum had already shifted by then. The nature of the beast had already changed.

Once upon a time, rock music was a medium for ideas and art, with commercial success viewed as a welcome, but not necessarily essential, by-product. Beginning around 1976, and certainly coming into full swing by 1978, the equation flipped. Now rock was a medium for platinum-disc-making, universal-cash-register-dinging, fat-cat-with-long-cigar-puffing superstardom, and if you failed in that direction, all the ideas in the world couldn't save you.

And you know what precipitated the shift? It was the very thing that so many bands had been pursuing all along: the mega-sales enjoyed by a handful of albums released around the cleavage of the decade. Be careful what you wish for. You may not know what to do with it.

Peter Frampton still beats himself up over the monster that he created.

"*Frampton Comes Alive* changed the music industry. Single-handedly, that one record. I am responsible—not for better or worse, for worse alone—I am responsible for turning the record business into an industry.

"Up to that point we'd been learning. Everything was new with rock 'n' roll, every year was new, everyone was having fun and making some money, and people got screwed but it didn't matter because you were having fun. And then, all of a sudden, all these people saw that one record or one artist could sell that many records in one go, and they got interested in the corporate world. That's when all the big mergers started, that's when all of that started." A sigh of regret, a groan of horror. "I am responsible." And then a laugh. "Although it would have happened sooner or later, so it probably doesn't matter."

He is correct. Records had sold by the bucketful in the past, but how big was the bucket? Two million? Three? Frampton sold ten million. It was insane! Numbers like that just didn't exist in the music industry. Even today, there are Beatles albums that have barely sold a fraction of what *Frampton Comes Alive* shifted, and that was only the start. Other record sales started going through the roof, and unimagined riches, sums that no previous artist (or even record company) had even dreamed of before, were suddenly there for the taking. It was only human to want to grasp your share.

Let's look at the albums that set these precedents:

Peter Frampton, *Frampton Comes Alive*. Beautifully produced (it remains the only live album that sounds like it could have been recorded in the best-heeled studio, without losing the sheer excitement of the show), a lot of catchy songs, and an inescapable gimmick (the talk box).

Fleetwood Mac, *Rumours*. Beautifully produced, a lot of catchy songs, and an inescapable gimmick (the band members' famously tangled love lives).

Eagles, *Hotel California*. Beautifully produced, a lot of catchy songs . . . Hmmm, I don't know about you, but are we sensing a pattern here?

Of course there's more to it than that. You need an artist who is prepared to work his ass off promoting the thing, and a record company prepared to spend a small fortune on marketing. And so on. But essentially what it came down to was, if you spend money, you'll make money. So people started spending money.

Released in 1977, the Electric Light Orchestra's *Out of the Blue* pressed every commercial must-have button there was to be pushed.

A double album when such things were at the peak of fashion, it was cut in blue vinyl at a time when that, too, was "the thing to do." In the age of superstar retreats, front man Jeff Lynne decamped to a Swiss chalet in which to compose his masterpiece. In the age of *Star Wars* and *Close Encounters*, the album had a spaceship on the cover.

And so on. It was desperately unfashionable to like ELO, but every-body did because it was impossible not to. You could loathe their music with every fiber of your being, but it still sounded amazing. Like an *orchestra*? Like an army of orchestras.

"10538 Overture," the band's foreboding debut 45 back in 1972, was a UK Top 10 hit; their self-titled debut album made the Top 40 and later in the year made its American chart debut under the title *No Answer*. According to legend, the group's US record company called manager Don Arden to ask what the record was to be called. Nobody picked up the phone, so the secretary delegated to the task scribbled a memo reading "no answer." Oops.

"Roll Over Beethoven" a rocking rendition of the Chuck Berry opus, characterized by an introductory snatch of Beethoven's Fifth, led off the group's second album, *ELO II*; the R&B-flavored "Show-down" led off their third, *On the Third Day* and, for a while, ELO stuck at least vaguely to its original brief. Versions of Grieg's "Hall of the Mountain King" and "Morning" appeared; lengthy, string-driven things sprawled across great swaths of vinyl; *Third Day* was even a concept album. So far, so portentous.

But then a tree fell on America's head, and suddenly ELO took off *big time*. *Eldorado* sold a million without any warning whatsoever; "Can't Get It Out of My Head," a lush pop pastiche fuelled by a thirty-piece string section, slammed into the Top 10, and by 1975, ELO were spending most of their time on the road, even as Lynne per-fected the trademark sound that would render every subsequent release readily identifiable and infuriatingly catchy. Cellos were cel-loing, strings stringing, mellotrons mellotroning . . . and cash regis-ters ker-ching-ing.

Face the Music consolidated the band's sound and success; *A New World Record*, in 1976, confirmed it. "Strange Magic," "Living Thing," "Rockaria," "Do Ya," "Telephone Line." Those two albums alone pro-duced enough to fill half a greatest hits album, but Lynne had only just gotten started. *Out of the Blue*, still readily accepted as one of the most overbearingly, overwhelmingly, over-the-top-ingly bombastic albums of all time, made number four on both sides of the Atlantic, spilling five mega-hit singles as it went.

From the soaring "Turn to Stone," to the driving "Sweet Talking Woman"; from the maddening "Wild West Hero" to the so-compulsive-it's-cruel "Mr. Blue Sky," *Out of the Blue* matched every sonic standard that has ever been revered as the peak of a musician's ambition. Even *Sgt. Pepper* sounded dowdy alongside it, and there was more to come.

Touring *Out of the Blue*, ELO were so adamant that nothing stand in the way of their artistry that swaths of their live set were prerecorded on tape, a move that aroused both critical derision and the threat, unbelievably, of legal action—unbelievable because today it's rare to find a band that *doesn't* prerecord vast chunks of the concert beforehand, to save them the bother of having to move. Across the board, ELO became a phenomenon; indeed, the sheer perfection of *Out of the Blue* was such that even they would never be able to follow it. *Discovery* was a bigger hit, but it was infinitely less memorable, and everything after that was cold custard.

But their legacy remained solid gold, because how could it not? What an ability! The power to transmute base emotion into passionless platinum! To take the primal energy of rock and convert it into the streamlined ambiguity of wallpaper, without anybody even being aware of the fact. Coldly, calculatingly, and very deliberately, the Electric Light Orchestra took the living thing called rock and turned it to stone, just like their old hit said they would. And no, you couldn't get it out of your head.

In strictly materialistic terms, Tom Scholz was nobody. He had a day job at Polaroid, and the tiny recording studio that he'd built in his basement was essentially scavenged from the same discarded household equipment that every other would-be Phil Spector starts out on.

Browse through his record collection, too, and there would be little to make your jaw hit the ground. The Electric Light Orchestra. Queen. The Doobie Brothers. *Frampton Comes Alive.* Led Zeppelin. Good stuff for sure, but the same stuff as every other kid on the block.

What Scholz also possessed, though, what raised him above all the other basement-dwelling bottom-feeders yammering through on three badly played chords and a prayer, was *vision.* Vision, and the patience to see it through. For six years, he and a handful of friends had been recording demos, initially at what Scholz recalled as "frighteningly expensive studios that cost more per hour than I could save in a week," but increasingly in Scholz's rapidly expanding basement workshop.

Nothing happened. "After years of knocking on doors with tapes in hand, I had heard 'not interested' expressed in every possible combination of words from the English language." So now he was giving up. One more set of demos, one more go-round the record labels, and that would be it. He'd sell his instruments, dismantle his studio, and use the basement for something useful instead. Polaroid would have his undivided attention once again.

Then he recorded *Boston.*

Some records are classics because of the songs that you remember. Pick up *Who's Next,* and the opening "Baba O'Reilly" and the closing "Won't Get Fooled Again" stand so high that their peaks would dwarf anything foolish enough to creep in between them, and the Who knew it. Solidly from near-start to close-end, *Who's Next* is the Who by numbers, four years before they deployed that as a self-flagellating album title. You cannot beat those bookends. But *Boston* was solid gold throughout.

The statistics alone are boggling. Buoyed by the sheer ubiquity of the opening "More Than a Feeling," *Boston* climbed no higher than number three in America, but the seventeen million copies it shifted were more than enough to establish it as the biggest-selling rock debut album in American chart history, a record it still holds.

Boston infiltrated every brain in the land. One surely scurrilous (and chronologically suspect) legend insists that ELO were so enamored with the album that it was Boston from whom they borrowed their spaceship, and it had nothing to do with Luke Skywalker & Co. Phooey. But another myth insists that Nirvana were trying to learn to play "More Than a Feeling" when they stumbled upon what became "Smells Like Teen Spirit," and there's definitely some truth to that one. But it doesn't matter. What does concern us is the sheer impact Boston had.

Boston did not reinvent rock in the mid-1970s. Neither did ELO. They did not even revitalize it. What they did was restructure it; realign the sound away from the hubbub of incessant live work and interminable riffing, into a world of studio perfection and bottomless budgets. *Boston* itself was the result of six years hard labor. "More Than a Feeling" alone took five years to complete. ELO worked faster, but there were more of them involved; plus, they'd been doing their jobs for so long now that they could probably do the final mix in their sleep.

The point is, the old canard about time being money no longer applied. Now, time *made* money, and if you think that's just me punning together a couple of Pink Floyd songs to be smart-ass clever, remember this: *Dark Side of the Moon* has spent longer on the *Billboard* chart than any other record in history. And it doesn't sound like shit.

Nineteen seventy-six was a classic year for monster records. Good ones, too. Dylan's *Desire* opened with his first genuine protest song in five years ("Hurricane") before winding on through some his most captivating landscapes in a decade. The Eagles' *Their Greatest Hits* wrapped up, indeed, the best of the nest. *Frampton Comes Alive*, Wings' *At the Speed of Sound*, Zeppelin's *Presence*, the Stones' *Black and Blue*, and *Fleetwood Mac* had all topped the charts over the past nine months; *Hotel California*, *Rumours*, and *Out of the Blue* were just around the corner, Pink Floyd's *Wish You Were Here* and Elton John's *Rock of the Westies* were still fresh on the shelves.

Elsewhere, Heart's *Dreamboat Annie* was a slice of fragile beauty far removed from the bloated travesty that the band would become, and so deliciously indebted to early Led Zeppelin that you could even forgive the group for the album's occasional clinker. Before joining the group, guitarist Nancy Wilson played the Seattle folk circuit, and the album's high points echo that discipline. Zeppelin, too, drew as much from the folk scene as they did from its amplified cousin, and that's what made Heart special.

Tom Petty & the Heartbreakers' eponymous debut so effortlessly recreated the twang of classic Byrds that when Roger McGuinn covered "American Girl," you could almost believe he'd written it.

AC/DC's *Dirty Deeds Done Dirt Cheap* featured original front man Bon Scott's most lascivious vocals plastered over his bandmates' most dissolute riffery. AC/DC were still finding their feet in 1976, two albums out of their adopted Australian homeland, and still being bafflingly lumped in with the first rumblings of the London punk scene by audiences who had never previously encountered such ragged hard rock stylings. But they were destined for grand things regardless. In years to come, AC/DC's fortunes would fluctuate as wildly as their music, from the heights of the post-Bon *Back in Black* to the lows of the late 1980s and beyond. But for the one-two punch of "Love at First Feel" and "Big Balls" (plus their debut album's "The Jack"), you could forgive them anything.

The Kinks were readying *Sleepwalker*, an album that restated all the band's old values from beneath the cloak of irresistible rock basics. Any of many earlier Kinks albums packed their share of shining moments, but *Sleepwalker* was the first in which the full set shared that sheen.

And Thin Lizzy's *Jailbreak*—quite possibly the last great rock album of the 1970s (which, in turn, renders it the last great rock album ever made). Released in early summer 1976, *Jailbreak* was Thin Lizzy's breakthrough LP, the record that ignited another eight years of superstardom. Later, a few sharp-eared observers would point out that its best-known cut, "The Boys Are Back in Town," sounded a bit like something Bruce Springsteen might have written, although vocalist Phil Lynott laughed such comparisons away. "I hadn't heard Springsteen then. I was going for that Van Morrison thing." It didn't matter, anyway. Springsteen was still stuck on the Jersey turnpike in those days, musically, if not literally. Lizzy, on the other hand, were going global.

So there was a lot of great music around and, for all of the British punks' bitching about tired old dinosaurs and boring old farts, a lot of really exciting music too, being made by artists who wouldn't know a safety pin if they had to change a nappy.

And within less than a year, it was all but a memory.

A whole new musical movement was erupting, not from the clubs and bars that were the traditional breeding ground of insurgence and energy, but from the studios where beetle-browed technicians played, and scientists reduced emotion to a row of zeros and ones.

Once, the only qualifications you needed to make a great record were a mind, a soul, and enough fingers to make your guitar sing like an angel. Now you needed the patience of a saint as well. And a heart that was cold as ice.

CHAPTER FOUR

Queen for a Day, or, Scaramouche, Scaramouche, Will You Do the Fandango?

In which we pause briefly to celebrate a remarkable band, the likes of whom we may never see again. At least until someone else comes along to rip them off.

IT'S THE STUFF THAT EXTRAORDINARILY perverse dreams are made of.

In late 1974, Sparks were one of the biggest bands in Britain. Two albums and four singles had, in just eight months, catapulted them from the ranks of underachieving also-rans in their homeland, to demigodlike household names in Europe. Front man Russell Mael and his Charlie Chaplin—esque brother, Ron, were the most distinctive faces in rock, and they stared out from every magazine cover on the shelves. Russell's voice, too, was unmistakable, an effortless falsetto that rattled off Ron's quirky, breakneck lyrics with a style and grace that was quite unique.

There was only one shadow on the duo's horizon. They had just dismissed their lead guitarist. So they did what any self-respecting superstars would do and began casting around for a suitable replacement. Someone well known, somebody respected, but somebody whose career was maybe on a distinct downward spiral. Somebody, the boys from Sparks decided, like Brian May.

It was the ideal solution. At that moment in time, there were just three guitarists in all of Britain who mattered. Mick Ronson, the now unemployed arachnoid lieutenant to Bowie's cosmic cowboy; Ariel Bender, the man who put the "heh" in Mott the Hoople; and Brian May, the star-gazing foil to Freddie Mercury's épée, five-foot-something of perma-perm style, with a guitar sound that could make your heart race.

But his band, Queen, had shot their bolt.

The press despised them. George Tremlett, author of the first-ever Queen biography, 1976's oddly titled *Queen*, reflected on the band's early years by remarking upon their "total rejection by the critics." Band publicist Tony Brainsby remembered being told by one heavyweight rock journalist that "he wasn't going to write about a load of poofters." Another paper even came up with a new category to lump them into. It was called "supermarket rock." Nobody, the Maels determined, could be happy trying to operate in that kind of environment, least of all a guitarist as great as Brian May. So they popped round to visit him.

It must have been a tempting offer. "I did like the band," May reflected. "I loved 'This Town Ain't Big Enough for the Both of Us.' Anyway, they came round, the two brothers, and said, 'Look, it's pretty obvious that Queen are washed up; we'd like to offer you a position in our band, if you want.' I said, 'Well, I don't think we're quite dead yet."

And does he have any regrets? "No, not a lot."

The Queen story is a saga of supreme persistence. Perpetual critical disdain and the occasional commercial blip, of course, are only to be expected in any band's life. Devastating illness and tragic death, on the other hand, are mercifully visited only on a handful. Queen dealt with both with supreme grace and bearing.

But what really impresses about Queen is, they never demanded that you took them seriously. People did, of course, and bound themselves up into Gordian knots trying to justify some of the band's most memorable moments, e.g., the video that portrayed Mercury as a vacuum-wielding hausfrau.

Queen themselves, though, just laughed and got on with it, and you can always spot a real Queen fan, because they know *when* to laugh.

How seriously should we take Queen? Not very, says anybody who ever went to see *The Rocky Horror Picture Show* immediately after attending a Queen concert. Tim Curry might have been a little more butch, it is true, but otherwise the segue was seamless.

Not very, agree the writers and cast of *Wayne's World*, who returned the preposterous purity of "Bohemian Rhapsody" to the top of the worldwide charts on the strength of three rather amusing moments in the back of a car ("Was it as good for you, dear?").

And not very, said Queen themselves, for how could you do anything but laugh at a band that would write a song about fat-bottomed girls riding bicycles? In anybody else's hands, "Fat-Bottomed Girls" and "Bicycle Race" would have been novelty singles. In Queen's, they became rock anthems.

They even had a singing drummer, for heaven's sake.

"We just did what we thought was worthwhile," explained Brian May. "There really was a terrible arrogance about us! But what that really means is, you're creating from the inside, rather than from an opinion poll. We never considered what people were saying as a guide to what we were doing. It doesn't mean we didn't care about our audience, because we cared deeply about them. But caring about your audience doesn't mean doing what they want you to do. It means treating yourself properly as an artist, so you are worthy of people's support. And if you're acting with integrity within yourself, your audience will understand that."

That integrity took the band down some remarkable roads, of course. "Bohemian Rhapsody" is merely the tip of an iceberg of almost godlike creativity, audacity, and, as May insists, arrogance. You can stop off on any one of their albums to touch similarly scintillating heights.

You can also split your sides laughing at the sheer madness of it all. But get onto the campuses of Middle America and you smirked at Queen at your own peril, because all the girls have fat bottoms out there, and besides, any band that could write the National Anthem of Idiot Sports Events must have had something heavy going for it. But hey, Mr. Football Captain! Why do you think Freddie named his band Queen?

Track through the first four Queen albums, and the entire history of modern music is distilled therein. *Queen I* is unabashed post-Zeppelin metal, shot through with just enough glamour to give the riffs some glitter. *Queen II* was half grinding rock, half airy concept, pompous enough to overwhelm, but earthy enough for you to completely discard your first impressions and make an absolute idiot of yourself dancing round the bedroom air-guitaring to "March of the Black Queen."

Sheer Heart Attack was their pop record, a succession of shimmering gems in orbit around May's showcase "Brighton Rock." And *A Night at the Opera* may have been named for a Marx Brothers movie (as it was its successor, *A Day at the Races*), but you dismissed its slapstick at your own peril. Because somewhere within, there was something you loved, and Queen had their fingers round its throat. One false titter and it was dog food.

Queen knew no shame. They stole from here, they stole from there, and in the magpie's nest of their scintillating best we find vintage rock 'n' roll, classic rockabilly, glam rock, sham rock, shock rock, schlock rock. Only Queen could get away with driving the '50s schmaltz of "Good Old-Fashioned Lover Boy" up against the vicious spite of "Death on Two Legs," because only Queen would have wanted to, and an hour in the company of their greatest hits brings up a dozen other, similar, sentiments.

But you only spotted the steals if you were in the same headspace as Queen. They didn't lift moods; they borrowed momentum. "There was no such thing as glam rock [when we started]," Brian May continued. "We were just a band who liked theatrics. We thought of ourselves as a kind of Led Zeppelin who enjoyed dressing up."

Few performers think in those terms any more. They have their role models and they ape them so slavishly that one can't even go pee without splashing the other's leg. The idea of taking something that someone else does, and then chasing it someplace else has probably never occurred to them—or, if it has, it is so swiftly dismissed by one adviser or another that they probably think it was all a bad dream.

Some bands are a doddle to duplicate. Remember the first time you looked at a picture of Steve Tyler and wondered why Carly Simon's microphone was dressed up like the New York Dolls? Or you saw Guns N' Roses and wondered why *they* were now dressed like the mic? It's the same principle. You look at the Cult, but you see the Doors. You look at Black Crowes, but you see the Faces. You look at the Spin Doctors and you think, How odd—Alexei Lalas has just joined Foghat.

Queen are not so easy. Yes, you can hijack the harmonics, but it's what Queen did with them that made them so special; arguably, the only band that ever came close to matching Mercury, May & Co. for great chorales was the Sweet, whose B-sides and album tracks are littered with layers and layers of glorious vocalizing. And who ever took the Sweet seriously?

You can lift the structure from one song, maybe two or three. But even the greatest cultural mimics (the Darkness just came to mind. Not sure why . . .) will eventually founder against the sheer versatility of the Queen machine.

It's like those sad-sack hair metallers who thought they looked like Keith Richards. Yes, he looks like a walking mudslide today, as his jowls crash down to where his guitar once hung, and you certainly wouldn't let him climb your coconut tree any longer. But Keith Richards rode through the late 1960s and most of the 1970s with a crinkle-faced charm that captivated generation after generation. He dressed like he'd suddenly inherited a thrift store, and had yet to decide what to wear and what to drape over the bedside lamp for atmosphere; and that trick he had of sticking his cigarette into the top of his guitar neck was just so fucking cool that even punk bands started emulating it. Plus, he made everything look so easy.

Fast-forward through absolutely any of the multitude of concert films and documentary footage that captures the Stones at the pomp of their prime, and it's guaranteed that you'll slow down when you hit the sequences featuring Keith, nodding out in a hotel room wearing the snazziest boots on the planet, grinning wildly behind Jagger's back as the singer tries to upstage his shirt. Even with his back turned to the camera, and his mind clearly in another room entirely, Keith Richards radiated cool.

"Well, if Keith can do it, so can I."

Fact: There have only ever been three men who could successfully pull off what the young Keith Richards did so naturally. One was Ronnie Wood, for fairly obvious reasons. The second was Johnny Depp, in *Pirates of the Caribbean*. And the third was the old Keith Richards.

Imitation is not the highest form of flattery. Imitation is the last, and sometimes the only, resort of the terminally unimaginative. When Britpop icons Blur emerged on a sea of rewritten Ray Davies songs, a lot of people compared them with the Kinks. The difference was, the Kinks weren't copying anybody. So, sorry to rain on your Coldplay parade, but whatever magic spark you're hoping will raise your band to a new plateau, you're not going to find it sniffing round the local used record store, wondering what the heroes of the past came up with when they were stuck for a word to rhyme with YouTube.

So stop it.

A couple of years ago, somebody gave me an Annie Lennox CD. "You'll like it," they said. "She sounds a lot like Freddie Mercury."

Yeah, maybe she does. But I liked the $2.23 that I got for it on eBay a whole lot better.

CHAPTER FIVE

Can You Hear Me, Cleveland?
or,
Four Ants Cavorting on a
Stage Seven Miles Away

In which we determine the day the music died, and find out whodunit as well.

I T WAS JOHN CAGE WHO SAID, "I have nothing to say, and I'm saying it," but it took stadium rock to hijack that equation from the cultural arena and place it into music. Great records, terrific sound, and utterly devoid of anything even remotely approaching a genuine emotion.

Here is a truth that I defy you to argue with. David Bowie once said he should not have been allowed to make records during the 1980s (and proved it by delivering three of his worst). He was not alone. *Nobody* should have been allowed to make records during the 1980s. Because, if they hadn't, then nobody would have been playing stadium rock.

To some observers, stadium rock is, quite sensibly, any rock being played by bands that were big enough to appear in a stadium, those venues that Brian May once described as "echoey arena[s], reeking of bull poo." And that was a disease that had been sweeping the American concert scene since the early 1970s.

The days when the peak of a group's experience might be rocking one or the other of the Fillmores were over. Ever since the Beatles turned established practice on its head and crammed close to 56,000 keening screamagers into the Shea Stadium baseball park in August 1965, local promoters had fought to out-gross one another.

Touring America in the late 1960s, a band was as likely to wind up at a high school gymnasium as a conventional theater, while the New Jersey live circuit of the day even boasted a very exclusive, private Catholic school, where gruesome monks and nuns stalked the corridors and the pupils' parents paid a fortune in the apparently mistaken belief that they were insulating their offspring from the evils of the outside world. An evening in the presence of Black Sabbath and *their* audience was probably not what mom and pop had in mind, but you can bet that the kids didn't mind.

As audiences grew larger, however, and bands' demands grew more extravagant, it no longer became practical for promoters to continue booking them into the kinds of venues that had previously served so gallantly. When the contract rider calls for more M&M's than you could fit into the dressing room, it's time to raise the bar. So they cast their eyes instead toward sporting arenas, the vast concrete domes and boxes that clung like carbuncles to the landscape, and they, too, quickly filled up.

Bands would do anything to make the leap into these venues. Guitarist Don Felder confessed that the main reason why he was recruited to the Eagles in 1974 was to help them make the transition from theaters to sports grounds. Before he joined, he explained, "a lot of their shows went well, but when you're an opening act for a big rock 'n' roll band, it's hard to go out and play 'Peaceful Easy Feeling,' 'Tequila Sunrise' . . . and 'Take It Easy' to a crowd that's standing in a stadium and have those people get off."

Likewise, although Fleetwood Mac built their mid-1970s fame on ballads like "Rhiannon," "Landslide," and "Crystal," it was the raucous "Go Your Own Way" and "World Turning" that resonated in the very back row of the farthest-flung bleachers.

And so on.

But though these bands, and all those others that crammed such venues, were certainly stadium (or arena) rock*ers*, they did not play stadium (or arena) rock. That term would not fall into the vernacular until a specific musical sound had developed to give it something more than a financial meaning, a sound born not in a fume-choked garage where past generations had honed their talents, but in the newly appointed super-swish recording studios, where supremacy was decided by the talents of the studio's own engineers, and by how up-to-date their equipment was.

Which meant how many "tracks" they offered, how many times a single guitar line or snare sound could be overdubbed without losing fidelity, how many vocal harmonies could be layered into one performance, and, ultimately, how *huge* a record could be made to sound.

Play Heart's "Dreamboat Annie" or Thin Lizzy's "The Boys Are Back in Town." Now play Foreigner's "Cold as Ice" or Toto's "Hold the Line." Mere months separate their creation in terms of actual chronology. But in terms of content, they are leagues apart. One sounds human, alive, electric, but also electrifying. The other sounds . . . how would *you* put it? Impressive, for sure. Dynamic, certainly. The drums are a symphony, the guitars a concerto, the vocals a choir.

But is it music? Or is it something else, some bizarre architectural construct mapped out on graph paper before being slotted together? It has a melody, it has lyrics, it has a foot-tapping beat. There's something there that you can't just put your finger on, though. Or, rather, something *not* there. It's called humanity. The sense that the song was written by a human, and performed by flesh and blood.

Move forward in time. Pat Benatar, "Heartbreaker." Asia, "Heat of the Moment." J. Geils Band, "Centerfold." That god-awful Cars song that kept turning up during Live Aid. Almost anything produced by Roy Thomas Baker once he got the first four Queen albums out of his system. Sound without substance, noise without nuance, a jackhammer for the senses, but *nothing* for the soul.

What was the day the music died? Don McLean rather pessimistically pegged it as February 3, 1959, when Buddy Holly's plane crashed into a frozen field in Iowa. Equally melodramatic moments can be drawn around the breakup of the Beatles or the death of John Lennon (February 1970 and December 1980, respectively), the birth of punk rock (summer 1976) or the emergence of U2 (their first UK single was released in May 1980). Peter Frampton might even say it was the day *Comes Alive* sold its first umpteen million.

All of these suggestions have a lot to recommend them.

Personally, however, I don't believe such a momentous event can be pinned to any single artist. Yes, it is true, as sundry addled visionaries have told us over the years, that one man *can* change the world. But *end* it? Even all-out nuclear war needs more than one finger on the button, and that's assuming that the glaciers don't melt first.

No, the music died on an indeterminate date in 1978, somewhere within that ten-month span during which the following albums fell off the new-releases rack.

> *Infinity* by Journey
> *You Can Tune a Piano but You Can't Tuna Fish* by REO Speedwagon
> *Don't Look Back* by Boston
> *The Cars* by the Cars
> *Double Vision* by Foreigner
> *Toto* by Toto
> *Pieces of Eight* by Styx
> *Hemispheres* by Rush

Eight classic albums, eight classic rockers (well, seven, because the Cars, lest we forget, were new wave), and eight slabs of such overproduced, overwrought, and overindulged awkwardness that even the "urgent" songs procrastinated furiously, while the slowed-down ballads simply sank without trace.

None of which would been a problem if nobody else had taken any notice. But all eight albums were hits. Massive hits, in fact. By the end of the century, *Infinity* had sold three million copies in the US alone. Boston sold seven, the Cars and Foreigner six apiece. The others moved eight between them. That's thirty million albums altogether, which is more than *Frampton Comes Alive, Dark Side of the Moon*, and the Beatles' first six US LP chart entries combined.

Those are staggering statistics, but it gets worse. Because where eight bands went in 1978, twice as many would voyage in '79. The total would double again in 1980; and from thereon in, you couldn't move for their vapid vapor trails. Nasty, ghastly, synthesized vapid vapor trails.

Technology is not evil. If it were, entire religions would have formed to protect us from Keith Emerson, and we'd have all melted down our copies of *Fly Like an Eagle* years ago. Besides, the explosion of early '80s synthesized acts that once dominated the British charts confirmed the instrument's place in the musical firmament. Their music might, to any educated ear, sound as if it's all just the result of a couple of stuck keys, but bands like Soft Cell, Depeche Mode, Orchestral Manoeuvres in the Dark, and Ultravox were essentially raised on synths, in the way that earlier generations were raised on rock. To them, the possibilities of the new instrumentation came naturally. Or as naturally as it can when you're wholly dependent upon inserting "jack plug A" into "audio socket B" before you can even play a bar chord.

Where the real problems lay, and where the music of the age took a seriously wrong turn, was when people suddenly realized that, although a bad song will always be a bad song, no matter how many times you sing the chorus, if you pump up the electronic drums a bit and run the keyboard part through enough microchips, you can pull the wool over a lot of people's eyes.

Or, as the engineer said to the power balladeer, "Your entire album sucks donkeys. But we'll fix it in the mix."

Technology has always had its opponents. The day the first electric bulb went on, somebody was bitching that it didn't smell as good as gaslight. The gramophone was inferior to performance, TV was inferior to the movies, music videos were inferior to actually figuring out for yourself what a song meant. And so on.

The first synthesizers had a frightful time establishing themselves in the rock scene. The Monkees were the first band to employ one of Robert Moog's little machines on record in 1967; Walter (now Wendy) Carlos was the first to win a Grammy with one (for *Switched-On Bach* in 1968); George Harrison was the first member of the Beatles to own one. And on every occasion, "real" musicians looked askance at the box of wires and tricks and asked where lay the talent in making a machine go bleep? The synth was a novelty, a little bag of pointless tricks that would burble and squeak and make funny twittering sounds while the rest of the band got on with the music. But Pete Townshend employed one to devastating effect across "Won't Get Fooled Again," while Keith Emerson built an entire band around the Moog's capabilities.

Soon, synths were everywhere, so ubiquitous that it is easier to remember the bands that refused to use them, rather than those that embraced them. Queen so famously labeled each of their early LPs with the pledge "No Synthesizers" that it was genuinely shocking when they finally released one (1980's *The Game*) that acknowledged that the instrument might have a purpose. The fact that Queen had long since passed their prime at that point might also have had something to do with it. Even they were getting bored with making the same noises all the time. The synth would allow them to make some different ones.

There was the preset that sounded like the wind, and which ignited Hawkwind's "Silver Machine" with such evocative aplomb. There was the one that aped an emergency siren. There were the orgasmic robot and the clattering locomotive. There was even one

Ten Artists from the '80s Who Gave the Decade Hope . . . and Why

Elvis Costello—Because the world really needed a new Bob Dylan. At least until he turned into the old Van Morrison. Plus, anyone who admitted that living through the '80s was like walking through treacle has to know what he's talking about.

Billy Bragg—In a decade of complacency and "I'm all right Jack" yuppiehood, Bragg was the voice of a generation's conscience. He even looked a bit like Woody Guthrie.

Bauhaus—They were tarred with the brush of something called goth. In fact, this is what David Bowie would have become if the '70s had lasted another three years.

The B52s—For fuck's sake, they were fun. Remember fun? It's what you had before synthesizers came along to ruin everything.

Marc Almond—And speaking of synthesizers . . . He emerged from Soft Cell, but was always more seditious than their synthpop sheen let on. Solo, he blended Jacques Brel with Lou Reed and kept on intriguing us from there.

Robyn Hitchcock—He's usually painted as an English eccentric, and his best work tended to update some fairly psychedelic moments. But hell, he wrote some great songs.

The Psychedelic Furs—Another of those bands that became synonymous with the big drum/big hair/big yawn barrage of the decade. Before that, though, for four solid albums, the Furs were the Velvets with even darker shades.

John Mellencamp—It's not that America failed to produce a single artist of actual note throughout the 1980s, it's just that I personally don't like any of them. And neither did you at the time, which is why you can only think of two as well.

Dire Straits—Nah, just kidding.

that sounded precisely like a wet fart. ELP's "Aquatarkus" turned that effect into a veritable symphony.

The synth marched on, together with sundry new toys. The Fairlight and the Synclavier were magic boxes that could replicate so many sounds and textures that, by the early 1980s, the British Musicians' Union was actively campaigning to have them stamped out. "Keep Music Live," the union demanded, and rightfully so.

Because, for every band out there that was doing something useful with the tools at hand, there were a dozen others who viewed it in somewhat more cynical terms. For example—why bother learning to play an instrument, if you have a machine that will duplicate it for you?

The consequences were hideous. From Loverboy to Bryan Adams, from Van Halen to Mick Jagger, from Yes to Elton John, that one big, brash, blaring barrage dominated the '80s rock scene and, no matter how impressive it might have seemed at the time—gosh, that drum sounds like lots of drums!—you simply couldn't shake the impression that Every Single Fucking Record Released That Decade was made by the *same person* pushing the *same button* on the *same machine*.

And, once they'd pushed them once and scored a mega-hit (because all hits in the 1980s were mega-hits; it's just the way people thought back then), they'd have to press them again even harder for the next one. You want to know why so many musicians in the '80s had big hair? It was to deaden the remorseless repetitiveness of their own music.

And just when you thought it couldn't get any worse; just when you truly believed that things couldn't get worse, they did. One final twist of the metaphorical knife, one last sly jab with the red-hot poker. Into the midst of our misery there came . . . the power ballad.

Now, if you want to be strictly analytical (and just a tad pedantic) about it, the power ballad was nothing new. Dip back to the much-storied likes of Aerosmith's "Dream On," or Zeppelin's "Stairway to Heaven," and they could both be construed as power ballads. They shared the same form, after all. A quiet bit, a loud bit, a vocal that yearned, and a guitar line that stirred.

But Aerosmith confessed to *Creem* magazine that they got bored with "Dream On" when they had to play it live, and Joe Perry's wife Elissa described it as her "bathroom song," the one moment in the set where she knew she could leave the room, confident that she wouldn't miss anything. And if that was their response to one song, imagine building your career around such things!

In the hands of their creators, "Dream On" and "Stairway to Heaven" were single shades on the palette, to be used or discarded as the artists saw fit. In the hands of the power balladeers, rising up on the orchestral sagacity of technological trickery, they were the only shades in sight.

Emerging from a swamp of manipulatively one-dimensional pseudo-emotion, power ballads short-circuited the psychic highway between performer and listener and, in so doing, rendered themselves impotent upon all levels. In the hands of a middle-aged, middle-class balladeer, singing his socks off for over-bleached over-forties on a swingers' trip to Vegas, a song like "Feels Like the First Time" or anything by Survivor would have been dismissed as a callously constructed tearjerker performed by musicians who should have been put out to grass years before.

But Foreigner had form. Foreigner had reputations. Foreigner were a supergroup. So were Asia, so were the Firm; so, God help us, were Toto, at least if you spend your time memorizing the contributors to old Boz Scaggs albums. People genuinely did flick on "Cold as Ice" and pay drooling obeisance to the Gods of Classic Rock. Because that's what they were. The constituent parts of Foreigner (ex— Spooky Tooth, King Crimson, and the Ian Hunter Band) were impressive enough to make your ears bleed. And what about Asia? Uriah Heep, Yes, ELP, and Buggles—er, Buggles?

And the Firm? Only past members of Bad Company, Led Zeppelin, and Manfred Mann. Ten years earlier, you would not have dared even *invent* a lineup like that.

But ten years earlier, you wouldn't have wanted to. And neither would they. For ten years earlier . . . No. We will not get into discussing personal motivations, musical ambitions, diminishing returns, or subzero bank accounts. Still, you looked at these lineups and what came to mind? Those crossover comics that Marvel used to do so well, with titles like *Giant Size Superhero Team-up*, and all your fabulous favorites on the cover: Spider-Man, the Hulk, the Mighty Thor, the Incredible Hulk, the Fantastic Four, Iron Man.

Except Marvel only did things like that occasionally. Foreigner and their ghastly ilk were for life. Or at least for as long as they could hold it together, and you needed only look at the musical journeys that the individual players had taken to comprehend the calculated desperation that had led them to their present circumstances.

From "21st Century Schizoid Man" to "Feels Like the First Time." From "Tarkus" to "Only Time Will Tell." You want to know how hard the mighty can fall? From "In My Time of Dying" to "Radioactive." That's how hard.

And if the veteran musicians were inexcusable, what about the kids that flocked to follow them? Like rats (or even Ratts) clambering aboard a sinking ship, Survivor, Night Ranger, Cinderella, Warrant, and Nelson all piled onto the slow train to synthesized somnambulism, until you could scarcely switch on MTV without drowning in a sea of the stuff.

Long silken hair, shiny sprayed-on trousers, T-shirts so tight you could see last night's dinner, and all of them aching and breaking and crying and dying, and tugging at the heartstrings with the merciless inevitability of Captain Hook's crocodile. It was horrible; it was beyond horrible; it was homicidal. And it all comes back to the vile synchronicity of the 1978 new-release schedule.

What was the day the music died? The day that I started hating new music. How about you?

CHAPTER SIX

Fat and Forty-Plus, or, Had Your Phil of Collins Yet?

In which our classic rock heroes reach a significant milestone, and every damned one of them belly flops gracelessly. Except for the singer from Genesis.

USIC JOURNALISTS RARELY get everything right. A lot of them don't get anything right. But every so often, the planets will align, the stars will smile down, and a prophecy will explode into such vivid Day-Glo glory that even your cat will start referring to you as Nostradamus. And you know how hard it is to get your cat to pay attention to you.

I discovered this in 1985 or so, when I concluded a review of the very recently emergent Simply Red with the words, "Money may not, in the words of their debut hit single, be too tight to mention, but follow-up material certainly is. Poor darlings, they really are doomed."

Six months later, the ineffably handsome Mick Hucknall led his merry men to the dizzy heights of number sixty-six on the UK chart, the first in a solid chain of British hits that would see them graze the very lowest rungs of the Top 68 on no fewer than five occasions over the next three years.

Vindication!

Of course, they had to spoil it somewhat by racking up another thirty or so singles that did somewhat better than that, alongside half a dozen chart-topping albums and total record sales in the region of fifty million copies.

But that is beside the point. Simply Red were not doomed because I said so. They were doomed because they were, simply, boring. Boring to listen to, boring to dance to, and, most of all, boring to think about.

Phil Collins, on the other hand, was never doomed. On the contrary, Phil Collins is the archetypal Boy Done Good, the kind of artless oaf from the wrong side of the tracks who, no matter how high the odds against him may be stacked, nevertheless discovers that everything he touches turns to gold.

His first band, Flaming Youth, should have been the extent of his career. They were young, they were pretty, and they got browbeaten into making one of the most absurd prog rock concept albums ever conceived, by the masterminds behind '60s pop supremos Dave Dee, Dozy, Beaky, Mick, and Tich. They were dead before they took their first breath.

But a passing acquaintance with Charisma label owner Tony Stratton-Smith landed Collins an audition with Genesis, at a time when they were so desperate to get on with their career that they might have picked anyone to be their new drummer. They chose Phil, Collins admitted, because he had the smarts to sit and wait while everyone else at the audition went through their paces, so he could figure out what the group was looking for. Then he gave it to them. He got the job.

Four years and four spellbinding LPs later, Genesis were again at a loose end, again in a hurry to replace an errant member. Only this time it was vocalist Peter Gabriel.

As we all know, Kevin Godley, Karen Carpenter, and Roger Taylor aside (and Ringo and Levon Helm if you insist), drummers can't sing. But Collins had harmonized alongside the departee a few times, and had simpered solo through a couple of songs. And no one else was cutting it, so they gave old Phil a go. Again, he knew what the group was looking for; again he gave it to them. He got the job.

It is very easy, if no longer quite so fashionable as it once was, to mock, knock, and generally dismiss Genesis' decision to upgrade Phil Collins from the very back row of the band to the very front. The shattering success that he has enjoyed since then has been such that even the old jokes about singing drummers ("What do you call a drummer who sings? A cab") have lost a lot of their currency.

Because it didn't matter what the fates threw at him—he just kept landing on his feet. His marriage broke up. He wrote an album (*Face Value*) about it, and that launched a mega-million-selling solo career.

Two of his friends invited him to join them at Live Aid. One of them was playing in London, the other in Philadelphia. It wouldn't matter which one he chose, the other would be jilted. But was Philip fazed? No, not a bit. He just booked a ticket on the Concorde and was able to play with them both. What a guy!

A homeless woman accosted him for a couple of pence to buy a cup of tea. He wrote a song about it ("Another Day in Paradise") and spent a month at number one. Can you even *begin* to guess how many cups of tea you could buy if your single was number one for a month?

Even when he quit Genesis altogether, after thirteen years nobly balancing his two careers, it only meant that when they did reunite, they'd be even bigger than ever. This man is so well starred that he could probably divorce his wife by long-distance fax and the phone company would wind up forgetting to charge him for it. Like wow, man!

Yet not everybody appreciates all that Collins achieved. Indeed, there are some people, grumpy old men in their forties and fifties for the most part, who still hold him personally responsible for taking control of one of England's finest ever progressive rock bands and transforming it into something that you wouldn't even bother to scrape off your shoe. You'd just buy a new pair instead.

Reinventing their sound as they streamlined their vision, Genesis cast aside their past as the faintly wacky elder brothers that every schoolboy wishes he could have, and reinvented themselves as '80s rockers *in Excelsis.*

No more the protracted epics about Narcissus, Slippermen, and biblical portentousness; no more dire warnings about property speculators, hogweeds, and headless Edwardian schoolchildren. Beginning in 1983, and lasting up until Collins' departure a decade later, the average Genesis song (and yes, most of them were very average indeed) was short and sharp. Samplers sampled, synthesizers synthed. Bizarre percussive effects chased the sound of "real" drums out of the door, and the button marked Bombast was gaff-taped down.

"Man on the Corner," "That's All," "Illegal Alien." Not since Kiss went disco and their audience went apeshit had a band executed such a dramatic turnaround. But Kiss recanted before the first returns hit the shops. Genesis just kept on going. "Invisible Touch," "Throwing It All Away," "Land of Confusion," "In Too Deep," "Tonight Tonight Tonight."

Because their fans didn't go apeshit. Or rather, they did, but their screams of protest were lost beneath the stampede of an entire new audience, hip little '80s kids who loved the dance floor stylings of this hot new limey trio. Who adored the funny little dance movements that Phil would scatter through the videos. And who enjoyed nothing more than turning out the lights and then scaring themselves with the roars that made "Mama." Genesis had always been popular. Now they were massively popular, but if you wanted to hear what they should have sounded like, you had to start buying Marillion albums. Because you weren't going to find it on any of Genesis' new records.

Genesis were not the only innovative heroes to be transmuted to imitative zeroes once the decade clicked over. Yes, too, were warped beyond recognition by the musicians' sudden grasp of new recording techniques and disciplines, and scored the biggest hit albums (and singles) of their lives. Nobody playing "Owner of a Lonely Heart" alongside "Close to the Edge" or "Yours Is No Disgrace" would ever recognize the same hands at work here, any more than someone brought up on "The Musical Box" would believe it was the work of the same minds that made "Illegal Alien."

But you were in the minority if you thought that the two bands would somehow be chastised for their duplicity, and a very foolish minority, too. Indeed, the more crass they became, the more the plaudits rolled in. Genesis titled their 1983 album after the chords that made up its title track. Yes responded by naming theirs after its catalog number. You and I might call that the death of creativity. The general public thought it was clever.

Half the bands that had spent the last half of the 1970s vanishing up their own backsides continued to do so, and were never heard of again. (At least until they reformed in the 1990s.) The rest just underwent such dramatic changes of musical heart in the new decade that you couldn't have picked them out of a police lineup.

Rod Stewart. Aerosmith. David Bowie. Bruce Springsteen. Bob Dylan. The Rolling Stones. Etcetera. Artists who had previously been so reliable were suddenly reduced to a bit part within their own legend. How long was it since they last, truly, went out on a limb? How long since they last cut an album that left their audience reeling in amazement? How long since they last had enough puff to blow out all the candles on their birthday cake?

The Big Four-Oh was zeroing in on everyone, an age that was unthinkable, maybe even unattainable, back when they were first scheming their stardom, but which had crept up faster than any watershed has a right to. A few had even passed the milestone, or were perspiring in its proximity, in the knowledge that, from hereon in, they were entering uncharted waters.

Other rockers had reached forty, of course, the rock 'n' rolling pioneers of the 1950s, to begin with. But they'd done so from the comfort of careers that had long since ceased to "compete" in the marketplace. Now they were content to grind around the revival circuits and casinos, rattling out their raves from the grave for audiences that wanted nothing more than a hefty dose of nostalgia.

The '60s and early '70s generation, on the other hand, still believed themselves to be viable performers. They'd survived thirty, after all, and there was a time when that had seemed unbridgeable as well. People still seemed to like them, as well. No matter how appalling you and I thought they were, Genesis' *Invisible Touch* and the Stones' *Dirty Work* went Top 5 in America; Elton's *Reg Strikes Back* was Top 20 worldwide. Bowie's *Tonight* entered the UK charts at number one. But whether anybody actually listened to these records or not is a moot point.

If there was life—vital, viable, artistic life—after forty, nobody had yet figured out what it was. When Roger Daltry announced that the Who's 1982 tour would be their last, *Rolling Stone* seized upon the band members' age as a prime reason why he was correct.

"Their generation is just another blip in the cultural memory bank. Hanging on to traipse the stage for yet another new wave of fans, they would run an increasing risk of becoming ridiculous."

Becoming ridiculous and sounding it as well.

At what point did the Rolling Stones decide to stop writing songs and start making noises that sounded like the Rolling Stones? You know, the Keef riff you know you've heard before, but which you can't quite put your finger on. The Jagger lyric that yelps belligerently about nothing in particular, before giving in to terminal Irritable Vowel Syndrome ("b'ttn ya coat, b'ttn ya lip"), the Bill (or post-Bill)—and-Charlie rhythm that thumps along with anonymous precision?

When did Steve Miller replace jagged edges with aimless soundscapes, and thoughtful lyrics with meaningless drivel? If you can't think of a decent rhyme for "Abracadabra," don't go using it in a song.

When did Paul McCartney suddenly realize that he didn't need to even write music anymore (1980's implausibly plaintive "Waterfalls" was his last great effort) because he made just as much money from banging out catchy jingles and giving the world a smiling thumbs-up?

When did Blue Öyster Cult stop setting cities on flame with rock 'n' roll and start worrying about "Lonely Teardrops"? (Actually, there's no need to answer that. It was when "Don't Fear the Reaper" became a hit, and they figured out how to keep remaking it.)

You could say that none of this really matters, that it was natural attrition taking its toll. Nobody expected miracles from Bobby Vee once the Beatles arrived; nobody mourned for Wayne Fontana and the Mindbenders once Led Zeppelin swaggered into view. The musical drought of the 1980s was nothing more significant than the old guard conceding that its time had come, and stepping aside for the next generation of fired-up gunslingers.

Only this time, something went horribly wrong. This time, nobody stepped up to replace them. Nobody worthwhile, anyway, and certainly nobody who could, as had always happened in the past, be promoted as a viable *improvement* on what had gone before. In terms of musical advancement and technique, the biggest band of the'70s, Led Zeppelin, were "better" than their counterpart in the '60s, the Beatles, just as the Fabs were "better" than Elvis in the '50s.

But who was going to out-Zeppelin now? Who was going to look back at *Physical Graffiti*, as Zep had undoubtedly looked back upon *The Beatles*, and say, "Okay, this is where we Make Our Statement"?

Duran Duran? Huey Lewis? U2?

Foreigner?

No. Sorry.

CHAPTER SEVEN

Basically, It's About the Essential Futility of Life as Seen Through the Eyes of a Man Who Thought He Had Everything, or, Tommy—It'll Tear Your Will to Live Apart

In which we get all misty-eyed and nostalgic over the long and tangled history of concept albums, and we wonder why nobody makes them anymore. Aside from the fact that they're probably too stupid, of course.

THE TECHNOLOGICAL CONVOLUTIONS of the past twenty years, from the death of vinyl through to the birth of the MP3, truly are a marvel to behold. Who could ever have imagined, as we lined up to be first on the block to own a copy of *Physical Graffiti*, that one day the only delay between a record release and your ownership of it would be however long it takes you to log onto a website and download the thing?

True, the thrill of possession may not be quite so profound, and you certainly don't get record sleeves like you used to.

In fact, you don't really get anything, do you? Just an icon on your desktop, and the knowledge that you just paid $10 for a tinny rattle that might become vaguely audible once your computer's stopped grinding its guts out, trying to access the program in the first place. Any other musical format, from eight-track to CD and onto 78, you can resell or regift or even recycle. An MP3 is gone in the click of a mouse. It's as though it never existed, and your purchase price with it. Caveat emptor? Bloody idiot, more like.

But we digress.

Record sleeves.

Famously, *Physical Graffiti* arrived in a multifaceted package that could keep you busy for days, and that was before you started devouring the lyrics and musician credits. Today, it's enough to know what a song is called, and even that doesn't seem so important any longer.

But convenience comes at an even greater price than that. The beauty of vinyl is that its contents were fixed into place. The artist would sit down at the end of the recording process, determine which track followed which one, what the first song should be and what the final one was, and then his instructions would be pressed into immutable wax, never to be disturbed. You buy a record and don't want to listen to track three, you have to physically get up and move the tone arm across the record (and run the risk of scratching it in the process). A running order was a running order, and, short of buying everything on eight-track, there was very little you could do about that.

Today, all you have to do is hit the Shuffle button.

Have you ever wondered why most new releases seem to start with the best song the band has ever written, and then descend into mundanity from there? Because albums do not have fixed running orders any more. The artist knows that you're going to want to hear the hit single first (or the hoped-for hit single, at least), and the rest of the disc is just so many B-sides, plonked on in the hope that you might like (or at least download), a few of them. But it rarely feels as though any thought has gone into it, there is no sense that the artist stayed up nights on end, trying to ensure that the fade-out of one track merged perfectly with the intro to the next. Because what would be the point?

Shuffle.

And, if it's bad enough that people do this with new releases, how much worse that they also do it to the classics. Because there are occasions when an album *needs* to played in the order in which it was first envisioned, because to do anything else isn't simply to distort the artist's vision, it's to demolish the very premise of the record itself.

That's the problem about concept albums. They're just so damned *finicky*.

Norman is a very normal, very unexciting accountant who believes that he's a major rock star, and sets out to write a concept album, based around his own life, that will prove it. His long-suffering wife is not convinced. "First it was a painter and a footballer, and ever since 1965, you've had this fantasy of being a pop star," she tells him, but Norman shrugs off her scorn. "I'm a star," he tells her. "And I've got the press cuttings to prove it."

It sounds very familiar, doesn't it? The original proposal for *American Idol*, perhaps? Or a day in the life of Sting? No, because it only *feels* like he's been around since 1965.

I know! It's . . .

Wrong, wrong, and very wrong. It is an admittedly hyper-slim summary of *A Soap Opera*, the finest Kinks album of the first half of the 1970s, and the putative sound track to a TV play that Ray Davies wrote for broadcast in Britain in September 1974. Even for watchers who didn't care a fig for the Kinks, the broadcast of *Starmaker* (as the project was then called) was a big deal, an indication that, finally, the two most powerful media in the country were coming together as one creative force.

Hardly surprisingly, it didn't quite work out like that, and wouldn't for another seven years, until MTV blah-de-blah-de-blah. What it did represent was the first time that two of the most powerful *dreams* in the country had come together, the merging of a rock concept album that was necessarily geared wholly toward appeasing the ears, with the visuals that the composer originally imagined accompanying it. And if that really doesn't sound especially appetizing, then obviously you enjoyed a very different 1970s from the rest of us.

The Kinks were more or less synonymous with concept albums at the time. Four years into the decade, they had already produced four solid slabs of vinyl devoted to one story or another. And why not?

It was all a long way from "You Really Got Me," "Waterloo Sunset," "Autumn Almanac," and "Village Green Preservation Society," of course. But Davies was relentless. "The reason I keep going is that I haven't achieved what I set out to do," he said; and what he set out to do was write a seamless set of songs that maintained a straightforward narrative from beginning to end, and didn't leave everybody scratching their heads by the end of track three.

In commercial terms, *A Soap Opera* was, sadly, no more successful than its predecessors, although it does at least stand as a landmark in the genre, as one of the very last concept albums that actually strived to be something more than it might have been (one more Kinks album, *Schoolboys in Disgrace*, and Genesis' *Lamb Lies Down on Broadway*, are the others). For what was once just a grand illusion, an attempt to raise rock 'n' roll out of the plebeian gutter in which it was born, was now to be transformed into something far more revolting than that: an attempt to raise the artist out of the gutter and into the realms of the immortals. There's Beethoven, there's Bach, there's Prokofiev and there's . . . YOUR NAME HERE!

Life imitates art. Building toward the climax of the 1974 movie *Stardust*, the hero, Jim MacLaine (played by a very youthful and impossibly handsome David Essex) responds to the sudden death of his mother by composing an opera dedicated to the deification of woman. It would be performed live and telecast to the world. "After this," MacLaine's manager, Mike (Adam Faith), told disbelieving business manager Porter Lee (Larry Hagman), "Jim'll be bigger than Adolf Hitler."

You can't say things like that today. When Bryan Ferry expressed an admiration for the architecture of Albert Speer ("My God, the Nazis knew how to put themselves in the limelight") in 2007, the headline hustlers went into overdrive; Roxy Icon Thinks Belsen Was a Gas.

People were less sensitive in the early 1970s. You could speak your mind a lot more freely back then, regardless of whether or not what you were saying was actually worth listening to. The Sweet even went onto British television's *Top of the* Pops with one of their number disguised as a Nazi stormtrooper. A very gay Nazi stormtrooper, admittedly, but the cameras didn't flinch from his swastika armband, and the Sweet were not blackballed by the Politically Correct brigade, either.

People understood parody in those days. They had a sense of humor. And they needed it, every time somebody announced their next record was going to be a concept album.

Jim MacLaine never did become as big as Hitler. He retired immediately after the broadcast, and he ended his days a sad overdose in the Spanish castle that he bought with his earnings. As a role model for any aspiring young rocker, with ideas above and beyond his station, Jim MacLaine was a disaster. But that didn't stop people from trying.

Revisionist history tracks back through the evidence of the early to mid-1960s and credits any number of albums with igniting the concept boom—surf guitar fiends the Ventures' *Colorful Ventures*, because each song had a color in the title. Phil Spector's *Christmas Album*, because every song was about Christmas. The genre didn't even exist yet, and already it was getting silly.

The Beach Boys' *Pet Sounds*, the Kinks' *Face to Face*, and the Stones' *Their Satanic Majesties Request* could all be considered conceptual via one stretch of the imagination or another ("We've written an album that sucks from start to finish! What a concept!"), although again, mere thematic sympathies are scarcely a coherent story line, and for every person who saw *Pet Sounds* as a remarkable insight into the mind of its maker, there was another who regarded *Sgt. Pepper* as an overblown heap of vaudevillian daftness.

The Who's *Sell Out*, too, had thematic overtones, all the songs on side one linked by spoof commercials to reflect twenty or so minutes in the company of Britain's recently outlawed pirate radio stations. But the first incontrovertible concept album was the Pretty Things' *SF Sorrow*, recorded at Abbey Road in spring 1967, at the exact same time as the Beatles were cutting *Sgt. Pepper* (and Pink Floyd were working on *Piper at the Gates of Dawn*), all in same building. Could you imagine such a thing today, three great bands recording three classic albums, simultaneously in one place? Not unless they were all sharing the same bedroom you couldn't.

The Pretty Things never thought of *SF Sorrow* as a "concept" at the time; the phrase did not exist then. Singer Phil May had written a short story, and now they wanted to set it to music, across the course of a full-length LP—unaware, at that time, that record company stupidity would hold the record's release back until the following Christmas, 1968, or that Pete Townshend and Who co-manager Kit Lambert had hatched much the same idea themselves, only theirs was even more grandiose. They didn't call it a concept album, either.

"Hey, boys, I've had a great idea for our next album. Four sides of music about a deaf, dumb, and blind kid who plays pinball and starts his own religion."

"Sounds great, Pete. Maybe I should take one of those pills as well."

Andrew Loog Oldham, the visionary genius who laid the foundations of so much that we value toay, tells us a story, in which Arthur Brown, the operatically tonsiled front man of an eponymous Crazy

World, recalls the night when Lambert announced, apropos of nothing, "I'm going to appeal to their snobbery."

"Whose snobbery?" asked Brown.

"Those people out there, the punters, the general public," Lambert replied, with an airy wave of his hand. "With this thing Pete and the boys have put together. I'm going to call it a rock opera. I'll get them hooked."

He was true to his word. The world was hooked, and has continued to be so, on more multimedia occasions than one even cares to calculate. *Tommy* the album, *Tommy* the tours, *Tommy* the Lou Reizner musical, *Tommy* the Ken Russell movie, *Tommy* the slap-it-on-the-boards Pete-goes-Andrew-Lloyd-Webber multimillion-dollar revival. As the *New Musical Express* paraphrased, during the mid-'70s rush of merchandising that surrounded the release of the movie, "*Tommy*: It'll tear your wallet apart."

Tommy was huge. It rewrote the Who's bank balances, and it absolutely rewrote their future. Townshend was so stunned by its immensity that he has spent great swaths of the past forty years, if not trying to recreate its magic, and then at least repeat it. First up was *Lifehouse*, a vision of such startling complexity that even he admitted that he couldn't pull it off, and salvaged its best songs for *Who's Next*. It would be 2000 before *Lifehouse* finally appeared, still incomplete, but neatly packaged regardless, within a box set that included demos, themes, experiments and a two-disc radio play. None of which really made sense, but hey, thanks anyway.

He returned to the fray in 1973 with *Quadrophenia*, a far more cohesive and enjoyable work than the overarching sprawl of *Tommy*, with a tale that actually held together through the songs, and a vision that worked all the better because it was so damned near autobiographical. Jimmy the Mod, so fucked up that his own father reckoned that schizophrenia only began to explain the boy's problems. "You've got *quadro*phenia."

Like *Tommy*, *Quadrophenia* would make it onto the movie screens, and the film, too, wiped the floor with its predecessor, sticking so strictly to the album's story line that it more or less echoed the pictures that you'd had in your mind all along. But we're jumping ahead again. Emboldened by the example of *Tommy*, Ray Davies set to work on the Kinks' first concept set, *Arthur (or The Decline and Fall of the British Empire)*, the tale of an ordinary man with an ordinary life, who ups and leaves his homeland for the new world of Australia. When that didn't work, he followed through with *Lola Versus Powerman and the Money-Go-Round, Part One* and, when that stiffed, tried, tried again. By 1976, even the band's staunchest supporters were pleading with Davies to release an LP that didn't labor beneath another of his concepts, that instead wrapped up a dozen or so great songs and let them exist within their own little universes.

For that was, and remains, the problem with concept albums. Not every song work. A plot is a plot, and the simple need for continuity dictated that occasionally, a less than Shakespearean lyric was required (usually attached to a less than scintillating melody), to move the story along. Even *Quadrophenia* had those moments where the plot slipped out of focus, or where an instrumental needed to step in where lyrics feared to tread.

Every now and then, the mold would be broken. Lou Reed's *Berlin*, chronicling the acrimonious collapse of a marriage, remains possibly the single most cohesive, and therefore successful, concept album of them all. Indeed, it is an indication of just how perfectly realized *Berlin* was that within two years, its unifying theme of divorce of a relationship had prompted both Bob Dylan (*Blood on the Tracks*) and Peter Hammill (*Over*) to follow through with their own personal takes on a similar calamity.

The principal arena in which the concept wars would be fought through the 1970s was the prog rock sphere, where the airy conceits that were already part and parcel of a band's musical arsenal could truly lend themselves to the expanded format. Emerson, Lake & Palmer, perhaps the band best equipped for such prognostications, ultimately proved more restrained than might have been expected; two conceptual pieces, "Tarkus" and "Karn Evil 9," ultimately spread over little more than a single side of vinyl apiece, even though many listeners disregarded the rest of the accompanying albums as filler.

But Yes (the galumphing—there really is no other word for it—*Tales From Topographic Oceans*), Camel (an adaptation of novelist Paul Gallico's *The Snow Goose*), Groundhogs (*Thank Christ for the Bomb*), and Nektar (*Down to Earth*) dived wholeheartedly into the format, while Supertramp emerged on the back of it, following two distinctly unimpressive albums with the more-or-less cohesive brilliance of *Crime of the Century*.

Even more impressive was Jethro Tull's contribution to the canon, *Too Old to Rock 'n' roll: Too Young to Die*. It was deliberately titled—of course it was. Anderson was pushing thirty, and his bandmates were breasting the tape alongside him. In an age when rock 'n' roll was still a young man's game, and punk was about to make them even younger, thirty was a gruesome prospect, for observers if not participants—"Hope I die before I go bald" and all that. But what goes around comes around. The thread of the narrative told of a washed-up rocker, rediscovered and reborn amid the wave of the latest retro fashion; and, if Tull were not exactly anyone's idea of the ideal candidate, still the guitars and riffs were louder than at any time in their recent past, the tunes were tighter, and the emotions more electric, and the title track was such a mendacious toe-tapper that it did the job anyway. No longer the po-faced princelings of horse-faced pudgy nightmare, Tull were reinvented as a band you could listen to without a degree in nuclear science, and by the end of the year, they'd even scored a UK hit single, with the seasonal "Ring Out Solstice Bells."

Jethro Tull stared the conceptual abyss in the face, then turned around to laugh about it. Rick Wakeman was not so fortunate.

The ex-Yes organ whiz practically built his solo career in the conceptual genre, not only re-creating such epic tales as *The Six Wives of Henry VIII*, Jules Verne's *Journey to the Center of the Earth*, and *The Myths and Legends of King Arthur* on vinyl, but translating them to the stage as well, and even adapting the latter for an ice-skating show.

King Arthur on Ice has subsequently become one of the most lampooned and laughed-about extravaganzas in the entire history of rock. Journalists have always been able to raise a cheap laugh by mentioning it, while VH-1 rated it number seventy-nine in its Top 100 "greatest shocking moments," up there with Freddie Mercury's death from AIDS and the vandalizing of members of Lynyrd Skynyrd's graves. Which may or may not have put it in proportion, but at least indicates the project's standing in popular culture.

Wakeman, too, probably looks back on it with mixed feelings, as the cost of the venture ultimately forced him into bankruptcy. But for anybody who actually witnessed it, who sat in an arena and watched as Arthur and Guinevere swore their undying love, and magicians and dragons cavorted around them—well, they probably thought it was rather silly too. But so what? It was a silly time, and if it wasn't Sir Lancelot sliding gracefully across a slippery stage, it was Keith Emerson strapping himself to his organ and then turning somersaults at the California Jam. Or Peter Gabriel taking the stage in his Slipperman costume, all lumps and bumps and vocal-muffling latex, to bemoan the recent removal of his testicles. People enjoyed dressing up, and they enjoyed having their idols put on a show for them. Which is exactly what Kiss did.

Other bands made concept albums. Kiss were a concept *band* and, for three years, from their emergence in 1974 until around 1977 or 1978, they were the greatest spectacle there was.

Perhaps the story that best sums up Kiss was related by producer Bob Ezrin, who oversaw three of their albums, beginning with 1976's *Destroyer*. He'd already worked with Alice Cooper and masterminded Lou Reed's *Berlin*. He knew what it was all about. The first time he saw Kiss, he knew what they were all about as well. Money-making nonsense. But one day his curiosity was aroused during a conversation with a high school kid.

"Kiss? Oh man, they're great. The kids at school love them. The only problem is, their records are so shitty. But we buy them anyway, 'cos they look good."

That was Kiss' secret. Musically they were little more than another stultifying heavy metal band, singing about sex, sex, and partying all night. Nothing special there. But visually they were the tops. They were Over-The-Tops.

Nobody knew what they looked like; they never appeared in public in anything less than full performance drag, disfiguring face paint, heels, padding, the lot. The guitarist fired skyrockets from his guitar, the bassist breathed fire, the drummer levitated. In between times, flash bombs like atom bombs would detonate across the stage, and the smoke from the dry ice would choke the first fifteen rows. Manager Bill Aucoin claimed it cost $10,000 a week to keep the band on the road. But every record sold at least a million, and there was barely a critic in the country who would even stay in the same room as them.

"The whole concept of Kiss is unlikely," singer Gene Simmons eventually fessed up. "The fact that we started in 1972 when the glam-glitter rock scene was dead [sic] was crazy. So was the fact that we wanted to grow our hair at a time when everybody else wanted to look like Patti Smith. Everybody became, 'Hey, we're just like you.' We didn't want to be just like you."

Kiss' showmanship was irresistible for the kids who flocked to worship it and bought absolutely anything so long as it had their imagery painted on it (pinball machines, bedding, comic books . . . but not golfing supplies, which is where the Jimi Hendrix estate would later go wrong); and for the band's own peers, for whom the sky was now literally the limit.

Showmanship was what made people go to Pink Floyd concerts, just to see the inflatable pig, or sent them reeling out of Steve Miller Band shows, stunned by the enormity of the light show.

Miller recalled, "We had this great big huge green laser that we carried with us, with the guys who ran it. And I mean, you know, it was like a real, serious three-inch-diameter piece of light, and it would hit two mirrors and split into four and eight, and sixteen and thirty-two beams, and pretty soon we would have a sculpture all over the arena. And we used to put them on mirror balls, which would fill the room with little white specks of light as they were floating in space. They made us stop doing that. They changed the regulations. But we were able to hook this stuff up and we'd go to football stadiums and, you know, put mirrors on top of their highest light poles, all along the edge of their upper deck and all over the place, and then we'd do light sculpture over the stadium. And if an airplane were flying by, we'd put the damn beam on the airplane. I can't believe we did that."

The Electric Light Orchestra toured with the giant spaceship that remains most people's most lingering memory of the event. Rainbow picked up a vast computerized rainbow, and that was just for a regular rock concert. Concept albums, which demanded conceptualized stage shows, offered up the greatest shows on earth.

Where it went wrong, then, was not with the overweening pretension that a growing number of journalists (and therefore their impressionable readers) began to despise—heavens, these things were pretentious all along. Nor with the equally overbearing sense of self-importance that now seemed to be as vital a component in the finished production as the lyrics, the music, or the pantomime jabberwocky.

It was the onset of the 1980s.

Pink Floyd, originators of so much in rock that was genuinely good, set the ball rolling, although it is only with hindsight that we understand just how destructive 1979's *The Wall* was. A decade had passed since the double album *Ummagumma* set new standards in self-indulgence by positively refusing to acknowledge that the package was nothing more than four slices of solo masturbation, slapped together with a makeweight live album; a decade during which successive LPs *Atom Heart Mother*, *Meddle*, *Dark Side of the Moon*, *Wish You Were Here*, and *Animals* set new standards in creative excellence, without ever vanishing up their own capacious rear ends.

But as Roger Waters wrested complete creative control away from his bandmates and set himself up as a musical version of The Man

Bryan Ferry Is Not Allowed to Mention, so the musical egalitarianism that allowed such edifices to be forged was demolished, to be replaced by another of such towering ego and self-importance that even *Ummagumma* was vindicated by its single-minded pursuit of its own egotistical hyperinflation.

The Wall was predicated around two basic themes: the trials and tribulations that life can throw at you, each of which becomes "another brick in the wall," and the isolation of the performer, illustrated on stage by the construction of a vast wall that ultimately consumed the entire stage and effectively rendered the band invisible.

Both of which were valid themes to explore (although you do have to ask the Poor Suffering Pop Star, if you really hate your job that much, why don't you find a different one?). Where *The Wall* crumbled in the eyes of fans who'd followed Floyd this far along was in its apparent rejection of the musical notions that had hitherto powered their music.

Whither "Echoes," whither "Shine On You Crazy Diamond," whither "Pigs"? Hell, by the end of side two, even "Several Species of Small Furry Animals Gathered Together in a Cave and Grooving With a Pict" would have been a welcome arrival.

But no, brief little song was followed by drab little ditty, and, with an audience that grew exponentially wider the more predictably dull the album became, the unthinkable happened: Pink Floyd were transformed from a glistening diamond in the crown of genuinely adventurous, progressive music to just another meat machine, grinding out precisely the same identically sized and flavored AOR sausages that had already rendered both their prog and pomp-pounding peers—Genesis, ELP, Yes, Barclay James Harvest, and their successors Rush, Styx, and Journey—intolerable.

Such bands once created what they believed was music for the ages. But their infallibility did not survive past the mid-1970s, and by the time the 1980s kicked off, it was apparent that even the greatest performers (like the tastiest sausages) have a very clearly defined sell-by date, and the world in which concept albums were considered a serious statement of intent adhered to those dates as ruthlessly as the most conscientious supermarket owner.

But what happens to all those boxes of cereal and packets of noodles that have exceeded their "best by" limitations? They get thrown away. Bands, on the other hand, can linger on forever. Ideas are more indestructible still.

CHAPTER EIGHT

Clapton's Still God, or, Would She Still Look So Wonderful If She'd Just Burned Dinner?

In which we ponder the ups and downs of a remarkable career, to prove that you should never lose faith in your oldest heroes.

LED ZEPPELIN MANAGER PETER GRANT was reminiscing about the time somebody told John Bonham a joke.

"We were at a party, and somebody came out with the one about 'What do you call a man who hangs with musicians? A drummer.' Bonzo walked over, towering above this guy, and asked, 'And what do you call a man who hangs with drummers?' Then he picked the guy up and swung him over the balcony, about twenty floors above the ground." Grant laughed. "I never did hear the punch line, but I'm glad the guy didn't say, 'Let me go.' Bonzo probably would have."

What was it about the '60s and '70s that spawned so many demented drummers? Once upon a time, the drummer was Mr. Rock Steady. Reliable Ringo, Charming Charlie, quietly spoken and turned-out gentlemen who would no more drive a limo into a swimming pool than they would dive into a ten-minute solo.

But then the worm turned. Viv Prince of the Pretty Things, Keith Moon of the Who, Rat Scabies of the Damned—trace the line of descent far enough and you'll eventually wind up with *The Muppet Show*'s Animal, and that, maybe, is what finally put a stop to the entire process. A guitarist goes crazy and his admirers cite Pete Townshend. A singer gets nutsy and he could be Iggy Pop. But a drummer? "Hey, man, you're just like the hairy one from the Muppets."

Bonham was exactly like the hairy one from the Muppets. Less deliberately madcap than Moon, less unpredictably destructive than Prince, Bonham radiated an unspoken violence, a sense that, even were he in a good mood, you really would not want to cross him. Peter Grant—himself no lightweight slouch when it came to safeguarding Zeppelin's various interests—had no compunction whatsoever about bringing Bonzo along when things needed to be sorted out, and the more fraught those somethings were, the better Bonham liked it.

His bandmates, Jimmy Page, Robert Plant, and John Paul Jones, were no less in awe of Bonzo than anybody else. And when Bonham died, there was no question in anybody's mind that Zeppelin died with him.

Not for Zeppelin the protracted, tragic zombiehood that awaited Keith Moon's survivors in the Who; not for Zeppelin the slow, sad decline that awaited the remnants of post-Morrison Doors. The moment Jimmy Page first encountered Bonham, drumming with folkie Tim Rose, he knew he'd found the only drummer he ever wanted to work with. And he never stopped believing that. Zep without Bonzo was never even a possibility. Well, at least until Bonham's son, Jason, was big enough to step into his shoes.

The Bonzo legends are legion. No Zeppelin biography can go more than a few pages without unearthing (or repeating) another anecdote, and the fact that most of them seem to involve copious amounts of the alcohol that would eventually kill him (the thirty-two-year-old passed away following an all-night bender) only adds further fuel to the remarkable aura that has built up around his life. Sort of eerily, too, for those folk who put stock in the weird near-coincidences that followed Zeppelin around, Bonham's death came little more than two weeks (seventeen days) after the second anniversary of Keith Moon's demise.

Coincidence? Or just freaky timing? It doesn't matter. However you view these oddly twinned tragedies, one thing was certain: The age of the musician as a stimulant-fired angel of manic destruction was over.

It cannot be easy being considered a prototype, to know that every time somebody tries to do something clever on their instrument, yours will be the name hauled out as the benchmark for which they are striving.

Once or twice, yeah, it's okay. A little ego boost before breakfast never did anybody any harm. But every minute of every day, it has to become grueling. Bonham was lucky: He *enjoyed* the liberty that his lofty status permitted him. Other deities are not so accepting.

Barely into his twenties, quiet and studious, Eric Clapton was an especially unwilling candidate. The most famous photograph of the young Clapton is found on the cover of the first studio LP he ever made, as a member of John Mayall's Bluesbreakers in 1965. The rest of the band are looking into the camera: Clapton has his nose buried in an issue of the kids' comic *Beano*. It was a playful gesture, but also a telling one. It spoke of a detachment from the reality of the life he'd chosen, and of a touching aloofness from the increasingly po-faced attitudes that were surrounding rock in general, and the blues in particular.

For Clapton *was* a bluesman. No matter that he was white and English—when he picked up his guitar, he was transformed. As lead guitarist with the Yardbirds, the best of the London R&B bands that arose in the wake of the Rolling Stones, he was the driving force behind some of the most exciting performances the British capital had ever seen, and that without seeming to even break a sweat. In any other band, the lead guitarist slashed and posed and made shapes for the chicks in the audience. Clapton, staring fixedly into a private void while his fretboard and plectrum all but played themselves, didn't seem aware that there *was* an audience. The kids called him "Slowhand," and the name fit him like a comfortable suit.

The spray-painting started slowly, somewhere around the time that Clapton quit the Yardbirds because they were growing too commercial (their third single, the surefire hit "For Your Love," was the final straw) for the more refined pastures of the Bluesbreakers. At first there was just one slogan, a scrawled "Clapton Is God" on a wall outside Islington tube station and, had somebody been passing by with a can of whitewash, it would probably have been gone by the end of the day.

Instead they passed by with a camera, and once the photograph was published, the graffiti artist's message took off. Soon, proclamations of Clapton's Olympian status were appearing on walls, floors, any possible surface, and as the touring Bluesbreakers drove into each new town, the race was on to be first to spot the waiting greeting.

And so, if Clapton had followed the crowd, it would have gone on. But he didn't. Increasingly uncomfortable with his deification, he came to dread the cries of "Give God a solo" that rose out of his audience. Consequently, the untrammeled virtuosity of Cream was followed by the mellifluous calm of Blind Faith, which was followed by the absolute anonymity of Derek and the Dominos, a band formed in the fashion of Canada's the Band, and named with an equal eye for avoiding the spotlight. There wasn't a Derek in sight.

But there was a "Layla," an eight-minute nugget that incredibly was ignored for as long as the band existed, but took on a life of its own once they'd gone. Released as a single in 1971, this ode to Clapton's lady love petered out at number fifty-one on the *Billboard* chart;

reprised a year later when the Dominos were dead and buried, it reached number ten.

In the meantime, Clapton just kept on playing. True, there was a hiatus at the dawn of the '70s, when he retired underground to work through the heroin problem he inherited from Cream. But from the moment producer Tom Dowd took him down to Miami and set about making God's comeback LP, 1974's still-effervescent *461 Ocean Boulevard*, it was clear that Clapton hadn't merely, finally, come to terms with his reputation. He wasn't especially fussed about it either.

Three albums that really couldn't make up their minds about whether they were laid-back rock or hyper-relaxed easy listening pursued Clapton through the mid-1970s; a string of sweetly memorable hit singles included the gentle reggae of "I Shot the Sheriff" and "Swing Low Sweet Chariot," a lovely breeze through "Knocking on Heaven's Door," and the oddly annoying in a but-I-still-like-it kind of way "Lay Down Sally." Then it was late in the evening, one night in 1977, and wife Patti—Layla—was trying to decide what clothes to wear. And Eric, the dear old softy, wandered over and told her it didn't matter. Whatever she chose, she looked Wonderful Tonight.

Let's not make bones about it, "Wonderful Tonight" is a horrible song. Not horrible in an "Uptown Girl" kind of way, but there is calculated schmaltz, and there is calculated *gushing* schmaltz, and it doesn't matter how heartfelt the sentiments may have been (we're sure she really did look wonderful; she was a beautiful lady who wore clothes like a dream). If you've never been trapped in a late 1970s discotheque, while every girl slow-dances with the boy of her dreams, and tries her hardest not to get her chewing gum caught in his hair, and he's thinking he might get lucky so now's the time to whisper sweet nothings in her ear, and she's wondering whether her dad will advance her a few bucks on her allowance so she can buy the new Dean Friedman LP, and "Wonderful Tonight" is flashing off the slowly spinning mirror ball—if you've never found yourself in that situation, then you have never been to hell.

And if you've never been to hell, then you managed to miss the rest of the Clapton '80s as well, because, having struck gold with one song that made pulling teeth seem a viable option, he now set about seeing how many more he could come up with. Then, when he ran out of ghastly ideas of his own, he brought in a collaborator capable of making even dentistry sound delightful: Phil Collins.

Collins produced *Behind the Sun*, the 1985 album that, politely, even Clapton's most devoted fans would rather claim not to have heard, than have to acknowledge how vile it was. By the end of the decade, it was probably safe to say that Clapton really had traveled as far as he could on the back of "Wonderful Tonight." It was time— please let it be time—for him to remind us what else he could do.

Which is precisely what he did. Twenty-four nights of concerts at London's Royal Albert Hall in 1990 allowed Clapton to reconnect with every musical thread he had ever pursued, a genius notion that may not have satisfied the baying of the disgruntled old-timers ("Hey, play 'Good Morning Little Schoolgirl,' you devil") but did remind us that, for every "Wonderful Tonight" there was a "Mainline Florida"; for every "Lay Down Sally" there was a "Presence of the Lord"; and for every decade that raced by in a hail of soft-focus AOR there was another that bristled with genius at every turn. In 1994, he even brought all of that awareness to bear upon *From the Cradle*, an electric blues album that caught him revisiting friends he'd not spoken to in decades.

Now that was more like it. Yes, there were still missteps—new albums that you'd play once and then file away until the day there weren't another fifty people queuing up to sell their copies on eBay, and awful collaborations like the one that united him with Cher, Chrissie Hynde, and Neneh Cherry for a UK chart-topping charity single. But, for every day that a fan might sit and wish he could turn back the hands of time, there was another day when it felt like Clapton agreed—agreed, and was capable of doing so.

A pair of blistering albums dedicated to his first idol, bluesman Robert Johnson. A heart-stopping performance at the George Harrison

Ten Guitar Performances Not by God That Still Transcend Absolutely Everything

Mick Ronson (David Bowie)—"Moonage Daydream" (live version)—LP *Ziggy Stardust: The Motion Picture*

Jan Akkerman (Focus)—"Hocus Pocus"/"Sylvia"/"Hocus Pocus" (reprise) (live version)—LP *Focus at the Rainbow*

Mike Oldfield—"Ommadawn Part 1" (from ten minutes into side one)—LP *Ommadawn*

Ronnie Montrose (Edgar Winter Group)—"Frankenstein"—LP *They Only Come Out at Night*

Felix Pappalardi (Mountain)—"Nantucket Sleighride"—LP *Nantucket Sleighride*

Gary Rossington et al (Lynyrd Skynyrd)—"Freebird" (live version)—LP *One More from the Road*

Jimmy Page (Led Zeppelin)—"Trampled Underfoot"—LP *Physical Graffiti*

Neil Young—"Like a Hurricane"—LP *American Stars 'n' Bars*

Marc Bolan (Tyrannosaurus Rex)—"Elemental Child"—LP *A Beard of Stars*

Robin Trower—"Can't Wait Much Longer"—LP *For Earth Below*

memorial concert in 2001, when he brought the house to tears with "While My Guitar Gently Weeps" (but maybe transcended the barriers of taste by performing "Layla" as well; let us not forget whose wife she was first). His organization of the Crossroads Guitar Festival and, in 2005, a reunion for Cream, which may have ultimately foundered for precisely the same bad-tempered reasons that the original band was sundered, but which nevertheless saw the group manage to get through its repertoire in one piece.

All of this he accomplished, and all of it mattered. Why? Because in an age where a musician would rather sample an old riff than try and invent a new one, where "inspired by" is simply a nice way of saying you're not capable of writing anything yourself, and where the guitar is regarded with so little affection that most of the bands who still utilize it are the ones that the media likes to tag as "retro"—in an age where all of those things are so painfully true that there really are people out there who think that the Arctic Monkeys have something to say, that Interpol are meaningful and Arcade Fire are so amazing, dude, sometimes you need to wind the clock back a few decades and remember when those attributes were earned on the road, not bestowed by a publicist. And granted to people we called heroes.

CHAPTER NINE

Weird Scenes Inside the Tar Pit, or, I've Got Eight Tracks to Hold You

In which your treasured collection of compact discs and your hard drive filled with MP3s are revealed to be so much wasted space, because every album that you really need sounds an awful lot better on eight-track.

WHAT IS THE MOST SATISFYING sound in rock 'n' roll?

Some say it's listening to the first two or three Rush albums on headphones, reliving those glorious days before Geddy Lee started to sound as untrustworthy as he usually looked. (Would you buy a used ferret from this man?)

Others believe it's an iPod stuffed with the complete Bob Seger catalog, or a CD box filled with Led Zeppelin live shows, each one highlighted by an even longer version of "Dazed and Confused" than the one that preceded it. Other still might think it's the Stones' *Exile on Main Street*, or sewing sausages onto Yes' *Tales From Topographic Oceans*.

Me? I think it's Paul McCartney & Wings' *Venus and Mars* album blasting out of an eight-track player. Imagine! Play it on CD, cassette, or vinyl and it rattles through its programmed magnificence, the soaring "Letting Go," the ferocious "Rock Show," the heartbreaking "Lonely Old People," without a care in the world. Play it on eight-track, though, and not only do you get all the wacky little grunts and chuckles that Paul and Linda put on there deliberately, you also get that metallic *thunk* at the end of each program, and the impervious rumble of the rollers and capstans as they grind the tape down to nothing. Aural heaven? The phrase hasn't yet been invented that captures that glory.

An eight-track, for those who live in a world without happiness, is one of those fat old tapes that you see in thrift stores, priced to sell and still not moving. You usually ignore them. Who wants a couple of dozen copies of *Frampton Comes Alive* cluttering up the house, even if you can't play them? Because *Frampton Comes Alive*, for some reason, is one of those albums you always find on eight-track. *Frampton Comes Alive*, the sound track to *Saturday Night Fever*, and something weird by James Last.

So why bother?

Because one day the eight-track will return to the forefront of modern musical technology, and the music industry will finally come clean. They've been ripping you off for twenty-five years. Vinyl? Scratchy, warped, and needs too much cleaning. Cassettes? Hissy, fragile, and they look like crap. CDs? Coasters with a superiority complex. MP3s? Great! I'll happily pay ninety-nine cents for *nothing whatsoever*. Eight-tracks, on the other hand—you know you've got a pocketful of something with an eight-track. Plus, they have the greatest sound reproduction you've ever heard. That's all.

Actually, that's not quite true. Reel-to-reel tapes have a better sound, but you need a degree in Fidgety Motor Skills to get them set up, and they're useless when you're drunk. Eight-tracks are simplicity personified. You pick them up, clunk them in, and, unless the tape breaks or the roller jams, they'll keep going forever. And once you're past the grinding, the groaning, and the loud metallic crashes, they have a clarity and dynamism that leaves DATs and CDs at the starting post. Which is probably why the industry began phasing them out in the early 1980s, at precisely the same time the first CDs were appearing. Nobody wanted the competition.

The eight-track takes its name from its innards, and to distinguish itself from the various similar formats that were developed alongside it in the mid-1960s. The simplest devices utilized two-track technology, and are best visualized as a length of tape that has been divided into two bands, lengthwise, each containing one mono musical program. Inserted into the player, the machine first reads one band; then, when it reaches a metallic marker at the end, it switches over to read the other.

Four-tracks, too, contained two tracks but, because they were in stereo, each of those tracks was then divided again. The eight-track, however, possessed four stereo tracks, requiring the tape to "turn over" at the end of each one, to bring us that glorious clunking sound.

In 1966, RCA became the first record label to adopt the format, when they adapted their entire catalog to eight-track. That same year, Ford installed the first eight-track players in all its latest models. Chrysler and GM followed in 1967, the rest of the music industry got on board, and hey, presto!—portable music was born.

Even the higher cost of eight-tracks when compared to LPs could not prevent the format's march forward. All of the advantages that were trotted out for CDs in the mid-1980s, ranging from portability and durability and on to non-deteriorating sound quality, were touted for eight-tracks, while fears that one's favorite records might not become available (a hurdle which the competing four-track was never able to overcome) were allayed faster than you could say, "Shit, the tape just snapped."

It is true that the eight-track was not the perfect medium for enjoying your favorite album. In the early days, record companies simply dubbed an entire LP onto the tape, irrespective of where the songs—and therefore the clunks—might fall. It is not unusual to find a song starting just as the program is about to end, fading out while the tape kerplunks over, and then fading in again.

This isn't always a bad thing. That marathon recounting of "Southern Man" that highlights Crosby, Stills, Nash & Young's live *4 Way Street* is so long it spreads across no fewer than three of the tape's four programs. And sometimes you wouldn't have the time to listen to the whole thing. Easy. Move quickly at the end of program one, punch the tape onto program three, and you can eliminate the middle section altogether.

But not every music fan enjoys having songs fading around like that and, in the mid-1970s, record companies commenced rearranging an album's running order to lessen the disruptions and, presumably, increase your enjoyment. Sometimes it was fine. Bay City Rollers albums, for example, were never conceived as continuous programs. But something like David Bowie's semi-conceptual *Diamond Dogs* loses all semblance of form when half of side two appears midway through side one.

Then there are those albums that simply *cannot* be divided into four equal parts without hacking up a vital moment; Mike Oldfield's *Tubular Bells*, for example, or something intriguingly monumental by Yes. Or those that, no matter how you juggle them, will never fit on properly. At first the manufacturers would do the best they could and then apologize for the blank space at the end of one program. But there was a solution: The majority of eight-track players did not, for some reason, arrive with fast-forward buttons, and you really can't wind them by hand. So someone dreamed up the bonus track instead.

Yes, the same bonus track that they were touting as one of the advantages of CD (when all they really wanted was a gimmick to make us buy the same album for the thirteenth time). Nothing is new. Pick up Elton John's *Greatest Hits* on vinyl or cassette, and you get eleven songs. Grab the eight-track and hey, you get twelve. Or maybe it's really eleven and a half, because the bonus track does fade prematurely. Or maybe it's only eleven after all, because it's "Bennie and the Jets," and that's already on the album. But the thought was there.

Little extras like that were a major part of the eight-track magic. Play your friends the *Sgt. Pepper* eight-track and see them gasp at the slightly extended version of the title track reprise. *Unavailable elsewhere.* Watch them thrill to Lou Reed's *Berlin*, with its thirty additional seconds of jazzy piano Muzak appended to the opening title track. *Unavailable elsewhere.* Then leave them in the dust when you casually put on Pink Floyd's *Animals*, complete with a full-length version of "Pigs on the Wing," a piece presented in two abbreviated parts on vinyl, cassette, and CD. *Unavailable elsewhere.* What do you mean, you've never heard it? And you call yourself a fan?

You want pretty packaging? Some tapes came with proof-of-purchase slips that allowed you to send away for any posters or booklets that came with the LP, while others were issued in their own unique boxes.

You want new music? Eight-tracks were still appearing (albeit in increasingly limited quantities) as late as 1988, courtesy of the RCA and Columbia House record and tape clubs. Among the very last releases offered were John Lennon's *Live in NYC* (1986), George Harrison's *Cloud 9* (1987), Michael Jackson's *Bad* (1987), and Chicago's *XIX* (1988). Not bad for a format that went out with ark, eh?

Most significant of all, though, you want pure sonic magic? Well, just play one. Better still, play a quadraphonic one.

Quadraphonic sound has gone down in musical history as one of the greatest and most expensive failures of the age. Touted, in the aftermath of stereo's so-successful introduction during the 1960s, as the next level in audio entertainment, "surround sound" was originally introduced in 1970 on eight-track, with the first vinyl issues following a year later.

The basic principle was simple. A regular album, let's say Pink Floyd's *Dark Side of the Moon*, would be returned to the studio for a complete sonic overhaul. Whereas once the music appeared on just two channels, the left and right speakers of your stereo system, now it could be spread over four. Sounds would be pulled out of the mix to be granted added prominence; some engineers even dubbed new effects onto records to increase the experience. An entire new listening sensation could be created and then played back through four speakers, each of which read just one channel.

Initially, the majority of releases, vinyl and eight-track, were targeted at the audiophile market, with classical and jazz albums high on the schedules. Gradually, however, the format broadened its scope toward rock and pop performers, with Columbia, RCA, EMI, and the Warner group's Elektra and Asylum among the most prolific issuers, responsible for remixing a stream of potentially big-selling albums in this exciting new medium.

Unfortunately, that was where quad's downfall lay. It was not bad enough that you needed to purchase an entire new audio system before you could enjoy these new treats to their fullest potential: Even worse was the fact that the industry had yet to standardize which of several competing formats was to be employed, with the result that anybody wishing to pick up releases from more than one group of labels would need more than one player to actually play them on.

Three major systems were developed and sent out to compete with one another in the marketplace—let the best man win and all that: Sansui's QS (quadraphonic stereo), Sony's SQ (stereo quadraphonic) and JVC's CD-4 (compatible discrete four-channel). A fourth system, Nippon Columbia's UD-4 (universal discrete four-channel) perhaps mercifully failed to make it off the ground, but still, those were confusing times. VCR and DVD enthusiasts will sympathize here.

Several labels remixed and released albums in two of the available formats; Virgin in the UK issued Mike Oldfield's *Tubular Bells* in all three. But these were the exception. In essence, if you bought one system, you were stuck with one group of labels, which was fine if you only ever picked up albums by Joan Baez (A&M and Vanguard both preferred SQ) but was hell if you wanted some Doobies as well. (Warner opted for CD-4). Had these conflicts been resolved, or at least become compatible with one another, quad might have succeeded.

In terms of new releases, quad was at its peak during 1975–76. By 1978, the whole thing was forgotten. But, no less than eight-tracks, quad abounds with some magnificent treats.

Bob Dylan's *Desire*, with an extended "Black Diamond Bay." Black Sabbath's *Paranoid*, with the fade-out of "War Pigs" played out without the speed-up. Alice Cooper's *Billion Dollar Babies* with extra added dentist's drill. Mott the Hoople's *The Hoople* with super-maddening Marionette effects.

And then there's Paul McCartney & Wings' *Venus and Mars*, whose eight-track quad remix was so spectacular that it is now being utilized for the DTS surround-sound CD.[1]

---

[1] *Venus and Mars* is a horribly overlooked record. For a start, it was the successor to *Band on the Run*, perhaps the one Macca album that is seriously held up as a rightful successor to his Beatles work. In fact, *Wild Life* and the pre-Wings *Ram* are both superior musical pieces but were damned for their playfulness, and for their proximity to the Beatles' dissolution. Secondly, it arrived on the back of "Listen to What the Man Said," which was a grisly ditty by any ex-Beatle's standards. But thirdly, and most importantly of all, it was the sound of McCartney having fun again, spinning off couplets—who cared if they were erudite?—getting as soppy as he wanted to and silly as he could, and really not caring a hoot for what the critics wrote because it was his album, and he was going to make it his way. And that's what really annoyed them.

But "Venus and Mars" is one of his most inspired slabs of balladry; "Crossroads" is one of his most uplifting covers; and though "Rock Show" might be Cornball Central, it resonates with everyone who's ever attended an arena concert.

Plus, while the album is great in stereo, it's even better in quad, and if you love the vinyl, the eight-track will blow your socks off. And there aren't really many McCartney albums you would say that about in public.

CHAPTER TEN

Hot Rocking Tonight, or, I Know, Let's Make It a Double Album

In which we continue our discussion of the CD's redundancy by highlighting another of their frailest failings.

THE PROBLEM WITH CDS IS, you can't turn them over. If you can't turn them over, then you can't count the sides. And if you can't count the sides, then you wouldn't know a double album if it bit you in the ass.

For the benefit of everybody who thinks that the format still exists, just because the Smashing Pumpkins wrote so many dreadful songs that they needed two CDs to hold them all (*Melon Collie & the Infinite Sadness*), the double album died a long time ago.

In physical terms, it disappeared when vinyl was first put out to grass, with the advent of CDs in the mid-1980s. But it was also killed in spiritual terms, when bands realized that a single CD could hold so much music that literally every last piece of crap they'd thrown together in the studio could be fit onto a disc.

No longer did they need to waste valuable golfing time cherry-picking the ten best songs from a stockpile of twenty-plus. Now they could stick all twenty-plus on there, and wouldn't the fans be happy?

Actually, no, they wouldn't. Because few bands, even good bands, ever have that many great songs put together at once, which is one of the reasons why the vinyl LP was always such a perfect format. Forty minutes—forty-five if you pushed it—and that was your lot. Anyone worth their salt could manage forty-five minutes of decent music, and if they couldn't, then what business did they have being in a band anyway? Sod off back to architecture school, and let someone else take your place.

Eighty minutes? If you could fill eighty minutes with music, then you must have had something really important to say. Because if you could fill eighty minutes, you were looking at a double album.

For fans of a certain age and above, the very words *double album* still pack a visceral punch. Because the release of a double album was an event, a milestone, a marvel to behold.

The Mothers of Invention released the first rock 'n' roll double, with 1966's *Freak Out*; the Beatles released the most famous, with 1968's "white album." Cream (*Wheels of Fire*) and Hendrix (*Electric Ladyland*) conjured epochal doubles from their wild imaginings. So did Derek and the Dominos (*Layla and Other Assorted Love Songs*). And every one was a masterpiece.

Double albums were rarities, reserved only for the most significant occasion—and that doesn't mean simply that the sleeves were great for rolling joints on. The Who's *Tommy* was a double, and so was *Quadrophenia*. The Rolling Stones' *Exile on Main Street* was spread across two slices of vinyl and, at the other end of the decade, so was Fleetwood Mac's *Tusk*. Genesis, *The Lamb Lies Down on Broadway*. Lou Reed, *Metal Machine Music*. Chicago, *MCMLXVII* (I can never keep those damned Roman numerals straight). Led Zeppelin, *Physical Graffiti*. Two discs, four sides, and multiple layers of meaningful magic.

But the double album's finest hour was when it was applied to a live recording.

Single live albums were great, don't get me wrong. The Rolling Stones' *Get Your Ya Yas Out*, the Who's *Live at Leeds*, Zappa's *Fillmore East*, Lennon's *Live Peace in Toronto, 1969*. All are up there at the very peak of in-concert incandescence. But you always felt a little ripped off by single albums, always wondered what else went on during that storied evening that didn't make it onto vinyl.

When Genesis released their first live album, the puzzlingly titled *Genesis Live* in 1973, the fan club whispered grimly of the epic rendition of "Supper's Ready" that was left on the cutting-room floor. When Pink Floyd included two sides of live music within 1970's *Ummagumma*, few people celebrated the band's decision to add a further two sides of studio recordings, when more of that magical concert recording would have been far more listenable.

Double live albums left nothing to the imagination; or, if they did, it probably wasn't worth worrying about. A few minutes excised from an overlong jam, a last-gasp encore reprising an overplayed hit single. A little bit more of the rock 'n' roll medley. No big deal. You buy a double live album, you're getting the deluxe treatment.

The best-known double live album, and the most successful as well, is *Frampton Comes Alive*. Released in 1976, at a time when Frampton was little more than just another rocker making medium-size waves on the American live circuit, *Frampton Comes Alive* leaped out of nowhere to astonish the world.

The lad was touring constantly at the time, and originally envisioned a live recording simply as a stopgap. "We'd done a couple of studio records, and nothing, but there was a nice following and the audiences would go crazy. Then suddenly we noticed we were the most sought after support band in the US, so we went, 'Wait a minute, the record sales are nowhere near as good as our ticket sales, so maybe we should give them what we do live.' That was the idea."

The original plan was to release a single album. But when A&M president Jerry Moss heard the finished mix, his first response was, "Great! Where's the rest?" So they put together another disc's worth of concert, and the rest, as they say, made history.

Frampton was stunned. "I don't think anybody could be ready for something like that. All of a sudden, I went from being this musician who did exactly what he wanted to do, and had for a number of years, who'd been allowed to make the good moves and the bad moves himself; I went from that to having all my birthdays and Christmases come at once. It was pretty crazy. Basically, I became the biggest act in the world." And *Frampton Comes Alive* was the biggest record on the planet.

Peter Frampton did not invent the double live album. He was, however, there at its birth. Six years earlier, while the Stones and the Who were still cautiously putting out single-disc documents, and only the Allman Brothers had broached double live territory (summer 1971's *At Fillmore East*), Frampton's tenure with Humble Pie was crowned by the release of *Performance: Rockin' the Fillmore*, four sides of vinyl dedicated to one of the finest live bands that ever walked the earth. Not every track was a classic, not every riff a gem. But when they knuckled down to the in-concert epics—sixteen minutes of "Rollin' Stone" and twenty-two-plus of "Walk on Gilded Splinters"— you knew why rock 'n' roll was invented.

The album was a reasonable success; laughingly, Frampton recalled hoping, on the eve of the release of *Frampton Comes Alive*, that this new album might do as well as *Performance*. "It would be nice to get another gold disc to hang on the wall." He ended up with enough of the things to build a wall.

Double live albums continued to percolate over the next few years. In 1973, Hawkwind unleashed the monumental *Space Ritual*, eighty minutes of brain damage recalling one of the most extravagant tours of the previous twelve months; the following year, David Bowie released the soulful *David Live*. Dylan and the Band brought out *Before the Flood* to try and circumvent the bootleg trade, and Deep Purple cemented their reputation as one of the world's loudest bands with the ear-splitting *Made in Japan*. Van Morrison fans said nice things about some of the playing on *It's Too Late to Stop Now*.

But the bulk of the pack still stuck with single discs, not only because they were cheaper, but also because most people, fans and

A Dozen Double Live Albums

Joe Cocker—*Mad Dogs & Englishmen* (1970) Ragtag souvenir of the tour of the same name, costarring Leon Russell and a sweet-sounding Rita Coolidge, and captured on film, too.

Deep Purple—*Made in Japan* (1972) Solid showmanship plus definitive versions of so many Purple classics that you can even forgive them the drum solo.

Lou Reed—*Rock 'n' roll Animal/Lou Reed Live* (1974) Two single albums released very separately, but that's only because the label didn't think anyone would buy them as one. Drawn from the same show, recapturing the same magic—you'd be a fool not to lump this pair together.

Mott the Hoople—*Live* (1974) Another single disc that should have been a double, and finally became one in 2004, when it received its long-overdue CD remaster. Shows in London and New York are highlighted, and the Bender version of the band is brilliant.

Kiss—*Alive* (1975) Distinct from *Alive* volumes two, three, seventeen, and twenty-four, this is the monster breathing fire from every pore, and really deserving the roars that come up from the pit.

Grand Funk Railroad—*Caught in the Act* (1975) Funk at their peak and probably the most essential LP in their entire catalog.

Lynyrd Skynyrd—*One More for the Road* (1976) Dramatic document of just how long "Freebird" could be stretched out for, without anyone even noticing.

Bob Seger—*Live Bullet* (1976) A solid encapsulation of everything that made Seger holy, and he'd not even released "Night Moves" yet!

Rush—*All the World's a Stage* (1976) It's also an idiot. Indescribably boring.

Genesis—*Seconds Out* (1977) Recorded in 1976 during Phil Collins' first year in charge, already missing the dynamism of his predecessor, Peter Gabriel, but still packing sufficient oldies to at least keep your toes tapping.

Rolling Stones—*Love You Live* (1977) Also vintage 1976, as the band toured *Black and Blue* with Ronnie Wood, the new kid on the block. Not the most essential Stones live record, but worth it for the El Mocambo side.

The Kinks—*One for the Road* (1980) While their peers all perished by the roadside, the Kinks marched irreverently on, riding a string of superlative studio albums that commenced with 1977's *Sleepwalker* and actually kept going until 1982's *State of Confusion*. Late starters to be sure, but maybe that's why they were so good.

bands alike, didn't really take them too seriously. As Frampton pointed out, what was a live album anyway but a stopgap between studio releases, possibly a contract filler, often a contractual obligation, and usually more of a passing fancy than a record you'd want to live with forever.

Of course, there was always a handful of overachievers. Santana, Yes, and Wings each gifted fans with triple live packages, as did the guitarless ELP and the pointless Chicago. Into the 1980s, and Bruce Springsteen would not be satisfied with anything less than *ten* sides of concert recordings.

Other bands cheated a little. Fleetwood Mac (*Live*), Ian Hunter (*Welcome to the Club*), and Genesis (*Three Sides Live*) could indeed muster only three sides live, and padded out the double with studio material. But that only added to the authenticity in a way. A full concert *plus* some optional extras. Thank you very much.

It is not for us to wonder just how live a live album might be. Famously, Thin Lizzy producer Tony Visconti insinuated that very little of the band's *Live and Dangerous* LP lived up to the first part of its title, having been largely rerecorded in the studio, after the fact. But vocalist Phil Lynott went to his grave denying that. "It really pissed me off people saying the live album wasn't live, that we went back into the studio and redid it," he told me. "We redid some backing vocals, that was all. Maybe a bit of guitar. Everything else, the rest of the stuff that people say is bollocks."

Besides, does it matter? Drawing from tapes that stretched back two years, *Live and Dangerous* is the ultimate document of Thin Lizzy as an in-concert act, and that is how it should be. Who cares for, or even needs to hear, a live album recorded once the band is off the boil? Where Bowie's *David Live* arrived one tour too late to truly thrill the fan club, Black Sabbath's *Live Evil* came one singer too late.

With the exception of *Get Yer Ya Yas Out*, the Rolling Stones habitually released live albums to commemorate the lesser of their live adventures, and while it was lovely of Steve Miller to release *The Steve Miller Band: Live!*, why did he have to wait until 1983 to do it, and remind us of "Abracadabra"??

CHAPTER ELEVEN

The Curse of Pepper, or, The Worst Record You've Ever Sworn Was Genius

In which we contemplate our slavish addiction to the past
and admit that sometimes even history makes mistakes.

THE STORY OF HOW THE BEATLES came to concoct *Sgt. Pepper's Lonely Hearts Club Band* has been told so often that it is almost biblical by now, the rock 'n' roll version of the Christmas story. Tired of touring, and tired of trying to compete with such seasoned road warriors as the Stones and James Brown, both of whom put on a better-sounding show than the Beatles had in years, the Fabs retired to Abbey Road Studios to reclaim their crowns as the Kings of Pop.

It was a masterful maneuver, particularly in that they promptly turned around and unsheathed "Strawberry Fields Forever." If that was what they could knock out in a few weeks, just think what they'd accomplish if they could harness only a fraction of the energy they wasted on the road and pour it into songwriting, song arrangements, song production. They were already the greatest band in the world. An album filled with "Strawberry Fields Forever"s would make them the greatest band in history.

Well, there's no arguing with that.

The problem is, they didn't make an album filled with "Strawberry Fields Forever"s, did they? They made an album filled with "Good Morning Good Morning." "Lovely Rita." "Getting Better." And "Sergeant Pepper's Lonely Hearts Club Band." Twice.

Credit where credit's due. "A Day in the Life" would have been monumental whatever Beatles album it turned up on. "With a Little Help From My Friends" was at least as good as any other song they gave to the drummer. "Within You Without You" was included wholly out of merit, and had nothing to do with trying to keep George quiet. And both "She's Leaving Home" and "Lucy in the Sky With Diamonds" had "number one smash hit single" written all over them, even if they did need to wait for Billy Bragg and Elton John, respectively, to cover them.

So yes, song for song, pound for pound, it's easy to see why *Sgt. Pepper* is so universally lionized today. After all, I can't think of any other album that is so finely balanced between songs you might want to hear again and ones that you wouldn't care if you'd never heard to begin with—can you?

But what about the actual *achievement*? *Sgt.* Pepper wasn't just any old album; the Beatles themselves said it was going to be special, and the Fabs don't lie, okay? They just don't. Besides, it was only a few chapters back that we were singing the praises of ELO and Boston, and admiring them for the amount of effort they sank into recording their greatest LPs. Okay, so the Beatles knocked *Pepper* out in a matter of weeks, as compared to months (or even, in Boston's case, aeons), but we've already established that time moved slower in those days.

Four months in the 1960s was worth at least three years in modern chronology, and, according to the technological standards of the day, *Sgt. Pepper* was so up-to-date that there are *still* bands trying to figure out exactly how they got the barnyard noises to sound so realistic.

But it was John Lennon, who probably knew what he was talking about, who said that if you haven't heard *Sgt. Pepper* in mono, then you haven't really heard it at all. Which presumably explains why the mono version of the LP has now been unavailable in any format whatsoever since 1968. After all, if an album is *that* good, you don't want just anybody wandering around listening to it, do you? They might form their own opinion of it, and then where would we be?

But wait! There's more! Look at that album sleeve. It *revolutionized* the concept of cover art—it really did. Even before you cracked the shrink-wrap, there were the myriad mug shots to pore over, a galaxy of faces cut and pasted in attendance around the Beatles by artist Peter Blake. And then you opened it up and got the first free cutout cardboard moustache.

Genius! Sheer fucking genius.

And when you placed the needle on the vinyl for the very first time, that sunny June 1, 1967, it was in the knowledge that, all across the western world, and through vast swaths of the rest of the globe, several million other people were doing exactly the same thing. An alien spacecraft listening in to the planet from somewhere in deep space would have heard the exact same sounds emanating from every corner of the Earth. "It was twenty years ago today."

So what? Who cares? In fact, who's even listening any longer? There are some songs that you have heard so many times that you could live for another century and never need to hear them again. But there are very few LPs that have the same effect.

From the moment the record came out, *Sgt. Pepper's* praises were sung to the sky, and it's like the old baseball canard, "If you build it, they will come." If you build it up enough, they'll agree. Run a poll of the Top 100 rock albums of all time, and if *Pepper's* not at the top (and it does occasionally slip, losing out to either *Revolver* or the Beach Boys' *Pet Sounds*), then it's close enough that you know the blip was probably caused by a hanging chad. And ask for an explanation, and

Pig's Purse from a Sow's Ear— Ten *Sgt. Pepper* Covers

The Beatles made a hotchpotch of it, so let's see how everyone else can do. Does it sound any better like *this*?

"Sgt. Pepper's Lonely Hearts Club Band"—Jimi Hendrix

"With a Little Help from My Friends"—Joe Cocker

"Lucy in the Sky with Diamonds"—Elton John

"Getting Better"—Status Quo

"Fixing a Hole"—the Bee Gees

"She's Leaving Home"—Billy Bragg

"Being for the Benefit of Mr. Kite"—Billy Connolly

"Within You Without You"—Patti Smith

"When I'm Sixty-four"—Georgie Fame

"Lovely Rita"—Fats Domino

"Good Morning Good Morning"—Peter Frampton

"A Day in the Life"—the Fall

you can already recite the answer yourself. As BBC DJ Simon Mayo explained, "It revolutionized music and what we expect from an album."

How did it revolutionize music? Note for note, song for song, it was no more adventurous than either the Beach Boys' *Pet Sounds* or the Stones' *Between the Buttons*, and anybody who claims otherwise is too simpleminded for words. It just had better advance PR, that's all. And ask yourself this: Those aliens we met a few sentences ago have just landed and, handing you a blank CD-R, have demanded to know what the fuss was all about. "Make us," they insist in their funny, squeaky voices, "a disc containing the very best of Beatle band." How much of *Sgt. Pepper* would you include on *that*? "A Day in the Life" probably. "Within You Without You" possibly. And that odd little snatch of sound that turns up on the inner groove of side two maybe. But apart from that . . .

Yet still it's impossible to dispute the impact that *Sgt. Pepper* made. L.A. studio engineer Bruce Botnick recalled borrowing a mono reference acetate of the then-unreleased album from the Turtles (with whom he was working at the time) and playing it to the Doors and producer Paul Rothschild "months before its release. We were all totally blown away by such revolutionary creativity. As a consequence, we were inspired to shoot for the moon" on the Doors' second album, *Strange Days*.

The Doors were not the only ones. Across the UK and American music scenes, *Sgt. Pepper* galvanized a generation of musicians to try and emulate the Beatles' accomplishment, sometimes slavishly, sometimes in spirit alone, but always with open acknowledgment that it was the Beatles who had made them aware of the studio's true possibilities. Across the psychedelic rock firmament, the art of taking mundane whimsy and transforming it into something meaningful and wonderful was given a major boost, simply because of what the Beatles had done.

But to what end? From the scorched wastes of the Stones' *Their Satanic Majesties' Request* to the semi-thematic links that held the Airplane's *After Bathing at Baxter's* together; from the timeless symphony of the Zombies' (inadvertently misspelt) *Odessey and Oracle* to the half-baked efforts of an underground's worth of wry psychedelic songsmiths, *Sgt. Pepper* sent everybody scurrying off to make the last word in sonic significance, and the best thing you can say about most of them is, they made a record.

But how much better things would have been (not to mention how much closer to the spirit of *Pepper* itself) if they'd made one that wasn't self-consciously beholden to *Sgt. Pepper*, if they'd simply followed their personal instincts and recorded whatever it was they'd been planning before the Beatles came along and laid down their dictatorial directive, as opposed to spending the rest of the year constructing a loop tape whose message still reverberates through the music industry. *Sgt. Pepper* is a great album CLICK *Sgt. Pepper* is a great album CLICK *Sgt. Pepper* is a great album CLICK *Sgt. Pepper* is a great album CLICK.

Still, it is a good thing that the Beatles are still deified today, and it is grand that *Sgt. Pepper* is still held up as the single most significant achievement of the entire rock 'n' roll age. Just think of the wretched calumnies that might otherwise be wrought were the position of Number One Greatest Album Ever Made by Anyone Ever to become as open to change and interpretation as other popularity contests.

For instance, when the British public went to the polls a couple of years back, voting on the greatest rock album ever made to mark the fiftieth anniversary of the national LP chart, *Pepper* scraped past Michael Jackson's *Thriller* with a mere 201-vote margin. Now, *Sgt. Pepper* is turgid, but *Thriller*? It might well be the biggest-selling LP ever made, and might well have spawned three of the most popular videos of all time (the title track, "Billie Jean," and Eddie Van Halen's masterpiece "Beat It"). But the remainder of the record was more filler than thriller, and if you really want to nail Paul McCartney to the cross of musical infamy, his contribution to *Thriller*, the duet "The Girl Is Mine" really *does* make "Good Morning Good Morning" sound grand. Right away, the very possibility of *that* being elected the greatest LP ever is enough to send you. With Desmond and Molly by your side.

Indeed, the longer *Sgt. Pepper* is held up as some kind of sacred benchmark, the less opportunity there will be for any latter-day talent to some day dislodge it. It's entrenched in the landscape, it's a part of the furniture, it's one of rock's vital organs. You can scratch it, you can dent it, you can abuse it all you want. But, for as long as it's up there, glistening in the firmament, the barbarian hordes of modern-day youth will never erect a false idol of their own in its place.

Because *Sgt. Pepper* might be tepid melodrama. But would you really want to see Radiohead take its place?

CHAPTER TWELVE

Grunge Is Gonna Change the World, and Jam Bands Will Save Us from Ourselves, or, Papa's Got a Brand New Shitbag

In which we stop blaming the '80s for everything horrible and let the '90s take some of the blame as well.

E ARE ALL ACCUSTOMED to the notion of being shit on by our idols. Whether it's a lousy record arriving just when we thought they were headed for glory, or an ill-judged remark about a cause we consider worthwhile, the very nature of stardom, and especially superstardom, is fraught with the knowledge that you simply cannot please all the people all the time.

Unfortunately, some people take such colloquialisms too seriously.

In August 2004, the Illinois Attorney General's office filed a civil lawsuit against the Dave Matthews Band and their tour bus driver, claiming the driver emptied the vehicle's waste tank while crossing a bridge over the Chicago River, and onto an architectural-sightseeing boat passing beneath. Passengers aboard the boat reported seeing a long, black tour bus on the bridge as they were drenched in raw, untreated sewage; according to news reports, approximately 109 sightseers, including the inevitable disabled people, senior citizens, a pregnant woman, a small child and an infant, were on board when between eighty and a hundred gallons of the "foul-smelling, offensive" waste drained from the bus, through an open grating in the bridge, and onto the boat.

The band's own publicist quickly issued a statement claiming management had "determined that all of the buses on our tour were parked at the time of this incident," a comment that was apparently forgotten by the time the Matthews organization came to fire the bus driver, pay a $200,000 settlement, and agree to keep a log of every place, date, and time that its tour buses disposed of human waste over the next five years. Which was the end of that, although one wishes that every group could be so responsible over how and where they dump their shit.

Throughout a career that spanned almost thirty years, the Grateful Dead established themselves as part of the landscape, so firmly entrenched in what we think of as American youth culture that, when it became apparent that they were finally preparing to relinquish that crown, there were a few years when we really were staring into a void. The fact that we were already into the early 1990s by then, by which time the actual quality of the Dead's music had long since ceased to mean anything, is irrelevant. The Dead impressed by their very existence, and because of everything they stood for.

Free love, free grass, free music, and an audience that was practically a tribe alone.

More than all the music, studio and live recordings, that the Dead released both during their lifetime and thereafter, more than their almost synonymous link with the hippie movement of the late 1960s and beyond, they represented community in an industry that might talk a lot about brotherhood, unity, and friendship but that has rarely gone out of its way to promote such ideals. The fans even had a name, Deadheads, and a code of honor that was as ferocious as that of the Masons; at the same time, membership was an absolute free-for-all.

All you needed do was buy a few records, attend a few shows, hang out with a few people, and you weren't simply "in"—you were home. There were some Deadheads who hadn't bought a new release in years, maybe a few who didn't even like the music all that much. But, forming a vast, traveling city, whose tents would be raised wherever the touring Dead touched down, Deadheads were a ubiquitous sight across the American '70s.

How much more natural could it be, then, that every new generation should want to share in that ubiquity? Particularly once the Dead began to slow down and life on the road began to be interrupted by trips to the doctor's waiting room.

The Dead, and more specifically the Deadheads, had always encouraged bands to form in their idols' footsteps, and by the early 1990s, there suddenly seemed to be a lot of them, all vying for attention.

Not was all were cast wholly in the image of their founding fathers. Where they merged was in a penchant for playing lengthy, improvisation-heavy live sets; jams, in other words, which quickly gave rise to the media-friendly tag "jam bands"—which, in turn, spawned more groups to jump aboard the bus until, unnoticed by any but the most sagacious observer, an entire festival scene had sprung up around the likes of Blues Traveler, Béla Fleck & the Flecktones, the Dave Matthews Band, and Widespread Panic.

For the most part, those other bands rose and fell with precipitous regularity—here today, gone tomorrow. But there was certainly a point in the mid-1990s where you could easily believe that an entire new generation was being raised on the self-same principles that make us grow all tie-dyed and teary-eyed whenever we think of the Dead.

The kings of this new universe were Phish, hightailing it out of Vermont to spread the gospel of endless solos and obtuse song titles across the country. *Rolling Stone* described the band as a "cultural phenomenon," and it was true—they were. Tour after tour, Phish were "followed across the country from summer shed to summer shed by thousands of new-generation hippies and Hacky Sack enthusiasts, [while] spawning a new wave of bands oriented around group improvisation and superextended grooves."

But right from the outset, there was something *wrong* about Phish. Or at least about their right to inherit the throne that the Dead were slowly vacating. The Dead evolved from the blues and then created their own psychedelic fusion by adding other contemporary moods to the brew. Phish developed two generations later, and they too would seek to create a fresh fusion from disconnected reference points. But whereas for the Dead the process was organic, almost accidental, Phish were somewhat more calculated.

The Dead stumbled upon what they created, pioneers in the truest musical sense. Phish would not have that same luxury; knowing that so much had already been done in the past, aware that the quest for true originality could no longer be embarked upon with a headful of acid and no other cares in the world, Phish were forced to search out their hybrids, then drag them screaming and often unwillingly into focus.

In purely musical terms, that boiled down to one primary difference, and one that would forever separate Phish from the band with whom they were most commonly compared. Phish had more influences than the Dead could ever have counted, but the Dead knew more about the ones they had. The Dead made music, which in turn became art. For Phish, art would always be ahead of the game. Or at least, it would try to be. For the most part, it was simply tedious.

Have you ever tried to whistle a Phish "tune"? It may have melody, it may have chords, it may occasionally stoop so low as to boast something approaching a chorus. For the most part, however, Phish concentrated on the same fidgety logarithmic equations that made the likes of Talking Heads, Devo, and Thomas Dolby so irritating in the early 1980s. It was music, after a fashion, but it was music that relied upon fashion to sustain it, and as soon as people stopped being impressed by epileptic chord structures and sub—Really Bad Jazz noodle soup, it plummeted from fashion and burned on the deck.

Phish would never encounter that particular ignominy, because they never courted the kind of fame that allows that to happen. From the start, and even at the height of their success, Phish played to their own people. They did not release MTV-friendly videos; they did not chase the upper reaches of the singles chart. They didn't offer their music up for inclusion in car commercials or have it placed over the last few minutes of a prime-time TV drama to add unit-shifting gravitas to a cliff-hanger finale.

They simply existed within their own little bubble and reopened the market for any band that spent as long tuning up as it did actually playing songs. Blues Traveler, with their flaccid recreations of the worst album ever made by the Moody Blues. Widespread Panic, who induced precisely that whenever you visited a friend and he played them without warning ("Hey, dude, I think your kitchen's on fire." "No, it's the new Widespread Panic album!"). And the Dave Matthews Band, who love their audience so much that they took their hippie principles to the utmost extreme and trademarked their name. Power to the people? No, dollars for the lawyers.

For while the jam bands were rising in the festivals of the Midwest, in the far northeastern corner of the country, grunge was stirring with equal alacrity, and for every Grateful Dead fan who hung his head in shame whenever somebody mentioned the name of John Popper, there were a hundred Neil Young devotees who felt just as bad when you whispered, "Eddie Vedder."

In the hands of Nirvana and Mudhoney, the bands that arguably ignited grunge in the first place, at least as something more than the disconsolate squawling of a hundred feeding-back bass amps, the music occasionally had its moments. Like it or loathe it, there is something instinctively *exciting* about "Smells Like Teen Spirit," even if it is just the walking ghosts of your teenage infatuation with Boston.

But investigate the Seattle sound further and what do you find? Pearl Jam, rampaging incoherently through a soundscape populated exclusively by a heady roar of recycled Neil Young riffs (how many times *can* you recycle "Rocking in the Free World" before somebody starts to notice?), and front man Vedder's incomprehensible yammering.

For a long time, I was convinced that the Pearl Jam song I was hearing on the radio was called "Hee-Haw, Yabba Yabba Yabba Yabba Yab." Then somebody told me it was really titled "Jeremy." How the fuck did they figure that one out?

In person, and in interviews, Vedder certainly had his head screwed on correctly. Without ever sinking quite to the same depths of rent-a-quote reliability as Bono & Co., he did (and does) have the most admirable habit of tying his boat to an awful lot of worthwhile causes and speaking out for all of them.

But he also had an unfortunate penchant for speaking the obvious a little too loudly. Upon hearing, for example, that 240,000 people once dialed the wrong number when attempting to vote for a contestant on *American Idol*, he suggested that the people who watched the show were idiots.

Yes, Eddie, but *not* because they called a wrong number.

Pearl Jam are the biggest and, by virtue of their sheer longevity, the best-known of the grunge acts. Soundgarden, appropriately named for a particularly ugly piece of modern art stuck in a Seattle park, were close behind for a while, and Stone Temple Pilots, a band that didn't actually have anything to do with the city, but who could pull off that trademarked caterwauling like northwesterners born and bred, came in third. There was also a tidy crop of singer-songwriters who may or may not have already been thinking of singing songs about their *own* pain, but who were now lining up to trade in their tranquilizers. Liz Phair, bemoaning past sexual experiences to a pile of cheapo amps. Jewel, a fragrant Alaskan beauty who had previously published poetry. (And we all know how much we *love* poetry.) Jakob Dylan, whose Wallflowers cut such uplifting gems as "God Don't Make Lonely Girls" and "Some Flowers Bloom Dead," but who drew the line at a cover of "My Dad's More Famous Than Your Dad."

Arguably, none of these magnificently recherché talents owed grunge any greater debt than that due to any musical fashion that the record labels all leap aboard and then hammer to death. But sometimes that's all it takes. On either side of the mountain range that shields Seattle from the rest of the country, the word was out. Grunge is Good. Angst is Art. "Sounds Like It Was Made in Seattle" was a license to print money.

Of course Nirvana might have rivaled them all, and probably would have topped the lot—and that despite a third album, 1993's *In Utero*, that effectively went out of its way to prove that the relative tunefulness of the preceding *Nevermind* was anything but a lucky fluke.

Front man Kurt Cobain was a good songwriter, as he proved when he stripped his music down to raw melody and Nirvana appeared on *MTV Unplugged*. He was an entertaining performer and he supplied good copy, at least on those occasions when a journalist wanted to talk to him about music, and wasn't just seeking fresh sensation to further fuel the tabloid media's peculiar fascination with Cobain and wife Courtney Love.

They may well have been the greatest band of the early 1990s. But when you clock the competition, so what? In the land of the blind, the one-eyed man is king. Even before Cobain's early death ensured that he would forever be known as his generation's John Lennon (when any other era might have pegged him closer to Pete Best), Nirvana were being feted with the kind of laudatory prose that is normally reserved for the most righteous rock royalty, which again proved either that they really were a wonderful band—or that an entire generation of fans and critics had spent so long scratching around for a good band to love that they were now willing to accept one that was only half good, because the alternative—the jam band scene, EMF, and Right Said Fred—was just too skin-crawling awful to contemplate.

So maybe Nirvana *were* contenders. But the arrival of that fearful Reaper effectively cut them out of the race, and no number of unreleased outtakes, unheard interview snips, Foo Fighters albums, or untenable conspiracy theories was ever able to restore them to contention.

For it matters not what death was wearing the day it paid Cobain a visit, the jeans and checkered shirt in which he was discovered, or the high heels and lipstick of unfounded rumor: The fact is, the day he died was the day that grunge went into the history books.

CHAPTER THIRTEEN

Neil's Still Young, Are You? or, Hang Him in the Hall of Fame (It's Okay, the Feet Will Stop Kicking in a Moment)

In which we look at the multitudinous ways in which a rocker can make a reputation for himself, and study the singular reason why they don't any more.

IN OCTOBER 2005, in the grand old English city of Liverpool (birthplace of the Beatles and of the uniquely talented Frankie Goes to Hollywood), a passerby made a grotesque discovery in an alleyway: the tiny, naked remains of what appeared to be a recently aborted infant.

Within not even hours—minutes would be more accurate—a makeshift memorial had sprung up at the site. The police were still on the scene, removing the grisly remains and searching the grounds for clues, as the first teddy bear tributes, floral wreaths, and handwritten cards sprouted on the spot. There was no public announcement of the find, no official notice whatsoever of the tragedy. But the mourners came, regardless, to drop off their sad reminders and heartfelt wishes.

RIP little baby, safe in the arms of Jesus. From someone who is a loving mother.

Or . . .

RIP little boy. God will look after you now. From a mother and her family.

Others addressed the mother of the pathetic scrap.

To the mum of this little baby, I pray the Lord will keep you safe and well and you will come forward.

From all walks of life they came, detouring who knows how many miles, to pay tribute to the sad bundle of lifeless flesh. Some may even have picked up a late edition of the local *Liverpool Echo* as they walked, but they would have done no more than glance at the sports pages before they made their offering. But when they did finally get round to reading it, one can only fervently hope that they took solace in the police spokesman's words.

"Stop grieving. It's only a chicken."

Rock 'n' roll is *not* a chicken. Several of its most storied performers may occasionally cluck like one, and it has certainly run away from a few fights, which is how the PMRC got away with smothering our record sleeves with warnings about bad language, and why you can no longer smoke when you attend a concert, even though it has now been scientifically proven (*Nature Genetics* journal, April 2, 2008) that lung cancer is a genetic condition and is only rarely associated with things like . . . oh, I don't know, smoking.

But rock 'n' roll has positioned itself at the sticky end of so many social battles that, long before it started getting involved in global politicking and saving the world, it had already established itself among the most powerful forces for doing good that the twentieth century had ever known.

Which is why it had to die. And, even more importantly, why it had to be seen to be dead.

The death itself was easy. Money can kill almost anything if you throw enough of it around. But there were always those renegades who didn't know they were dead; "terrorists," we'd call them in this brave new world of ours, although the more romantically inclined might prefer to label them "freedom fighters."

Rock music is a part of the entertainment industry. Always has been, always will be. But it lurked on the outside, a minority craze for a minority of weirdos, all shooting up and shooting off on their own peculiar little targets. For every Billy Joel there was a Frank Zappa. For every James Taylor there was a Jim Morrison. For every Seals & Crofts there was a Black Oak Arkansas.

What was needed was something that would unite everybody in a single cause. Something that would prove that there was gold at the end of the rainbow, even if you hadn't scored a single hit record for years. A reward for good behavior. A Rock and Roll Hall of Fame.

And the fact that they spelt it like, with an *and* instead of an 'n', just shows how clueless they were. "Rock and Roll?" Thanks, but if I need elocution lessons, I'll ask for them.

No matter that the institution was the brainchild of one of popular music's most respected legends, Atlantic Records chief Ahmet Ertegun, who saw it as a brick-and-mortar memorial to all those unsung heroes who are otherwise remembered on vinyl and in newsprint alone. To cynics (and there are plenty), the Rock and Roll Hall of Fame was just one more in the ever-expanding roster of self-congratulatory enterprises over which the American entertainment industry has obsessed, ever since baseball inducted its first Hall-of-Famer in 1939.

There's a Golf Hall of Fame and a Rodeo Hall of Fame and, given the distinctly downmarket nature of the entire concept, there's probably a Mobile Home Park Hall of Fame as well, probably planted in the heart of Tornado Alley, because that's just the way things are today. Good for them. I'm pleased. They deserve it.

But a Rock and Roll Hall of Fame? I'm sorry, but what does that mean? And what, exactly, are the criteria?

For Maximum Consumption of Hard Drugs While Continuing to Look So Cool . . . For Piling More Expensive Limos Into a Swimming Pool While Out of His Skull on 'Ludes . . .

For Exhausting the Plaster Casters' Supply of Molding Material . . .

For Blowing His Entire Advance on Toot, but Still Bringing the Album in on Time . . .

And this is the big one: *For Telling The Man to Stick It up His Ass.* Yeah, rock 'nnnnnnnnnnnnnnnnnnnnnnnnnnnnnn' *roll*, baby.

You know? I could really get into this. In 1967, Mick Jagger, Keith Richards, and Marianne Faithfull were surprised by a police raid on Richards' country home. Marianne, the police later said, was naked beneath a fur rug. And rumor had it that a half-eaten Mars Bar was somewhere in the vicinity.

The furor was immediate. Nudity! Depravity! Obscenity! Candy bars! Even a half-wit could put that lot together to create a delicious scenario, and the story whipped around so fast that, shooting Mick Jagger's *Performance* movie debut the following year, director Nic Roeg included one scene that suggested Mick had the same candies delivered to his doorstep every morning.

Hey, man, you can join *my* Hall of Fame whenever you like.

But they don't make scandals like that any more. Thirty years later, singer George Michael was charged with gross indecency after allegedly pointing his tackle toward an undercover cop. Hmmm, Mars Bars or masturbation? Fur rugs or furtive exposure? Use your imagination, for heaven's sake. If you can't stage-manage a decent sex scandal, how the hell can you expect to make a decent bloody record?

Hell, you don't even hear good *rumors* any longer! When was the last time you were told, in strictest confidence, that so-and-so was going to have a sex change (sorry, "gender reassignment") so he could marry his drummer? That he'd had to have his stomach pumped after blowing a shipload of sailors? That he needed to fly to Switzerland every year to have his blood replaced? That he'd fathered forty-three babies by twenty-six different women, and every one of them had been sacrificed to Beelzebub in return for another platinum disc?

You don't hear any of that any longer, and life is all the more boring because of that. I don't care that the orchid-eyed Britney shaved her head so she could look more like Michael Stipe. We need our reprobates, we need our delinquents, we need our antiheroes. Because if we don't get them, what's the Hall of Fame going to look like in another twenty-five years? After all, how many bands can you nominate purely on the grounds of them being unctuous lickspittles? "Wow, man, that was the best corporate blow job I've ever seen. Do you think you could show me how to do it?"

They'll probably have to start rewarding longevity instead.

Oh, shit.

With a performer needing to have amassed a minimum of twenty-five years of frontline service, the Rock and Roll Hall of Fame held its first induction ceremony in 1986, welcoming the cream of the very first wave of hip-swinging, granny-scaring, long-haired barbarians into its midst: Chuck Berry and Jerry Lee Lewis, who'd both lived long enough to be there, and Elvis and Buddy Holly, who hadn't. Nineteen eighty-seven recognized the doo-wop and early soul eras; 1988 brought the first acknowledgment of "modern" rock, as the Beatles, the Beach Boys, and Bob Dylan were brought into the fold.

The two decades since then have seen induction spread far and wide across the musical spectrum, although not so broadly that some artists are not now serial inductees (Eric Clapton has been brought on board three times), and not in an especially timely fashion, either. The Dave Clark Five's Mike Smith was not the first artist to pass away on the eve of his induction (in 2008), but he sure cut it fine.

It was a narrow escape, to be sure. But the tragic thing is, he probably wouldn't have thought of it in those terms. For the one thing that seemingly unites every man and woman who steps up on that stage to be welcomed is, they are *smiling*. They look *happy*. They seem genuinely humbled and gratified that, after so long traveling from toilet to trench, they are finally receiving the recognition of their peers.

Instead, presumably, of being invited to all their parties and taken into the back room to do a line of coke. Yeah, the Hall of Fame is much more fun.

Sometimes you imagine that all it would take would be for one respectable rocker, someone with a conscience and the balls to buck the system, to loudly tell the Hall-of-Famers to stick their silly induction where the monkey stuck its nuts. And the entire edifice . . . Well, it might not crumble like ninepins, because it's too firmly embedded in the corporate calendar for that. But it might give the rest of us a glimmer of hope, that the values that once were flown like a freak flag still mean *something* to *someone*.

The Sex Pistols proved that when they responded to their 2006 invitation with the words, "We're not your monkeys; we're not coming. You're not paying attention." The Hall of Fame, their handwritten note insisted, was "urine in wine" and, while guitarist Steve Jones later suggested it would have been far more "punky" if the Pistols had played, the rejection was still worth its weight in gold. And it will remain so until they're as old and senile as the rest of the pack, and can be lined meekly up on a stage stuffed with stars while the fight is ripped out of them, the balls are ripped off of them, and then we can plug electrodes into their brains and have them film public service announcements about the health risks of farting.

Not that every inductee is to be pitied. Some have, in fact, devoted their entire careers to doing precisely what a decent rock star is meant to do; ducking and diving and weaving and waving, and basically going out of their way to make life as uncomfortable as they can for all those people who think they know exactly where they stand.

Lou Reed surely snickered into his hand when the Velvet Underground was inducted in 1996, if only because he knew that there was scarcely an industry veteran in the room who'd have pissed on the band if they were burning. For the Velvets, induction was less of an honor than a begrudging acknowledgement that history is not always rewritten by the winners.

The Alternate Rock and Roll Hall of Fame: for Services to Knowing What Rock and Roll Is Really All About

David Peel—Best remembered for his dalliance with John and Yoko, but responsible, too, for *The American Revolution*, one of the most caustic of all contemporary commentaries on late '60s youth politics.

Wild Man Fischer—An occasional Frank Zappa protégé, wild by name and by nurture.

The Mothers of Invention—Whose first three albums may alternate between the grueling and the grotesque, and whose subsequent career may have been one aural panic attack after another. But at least they were never boring.

The Pretty Things—Born again and again and again and again, and still making records today (2007's *Balboa Island*) that are as great as the ones they were making in 1965 (*The Pretty Things*).

Gary Glitter—He wrote "Rock and Roll." What other reason could there be?

Lemmy—When Motorhead first came together, even their record company wouldn't release their music. Today they're an institution, and Lemmy's warts kick ass.

John Sinclair—Author of *Guitar Army*, the most significant rock manifesto of the twentieth century, and sometime mentor of the MC5.

Vince Taylor—The author of "Brand New Cadillac" later declared himself to be Jesus, and exited stage left in a white sheet.

Yoko Ono—For finally ridding us of the Beatles. Sorry.

Eddie, the Iron Maiden mascot—Had a face like Margaret Thatcher and a body like Michael Jackson. But did any band ever have a more stylish icon than Eddie?

Two-time Hall of Fame inductee Neil Young, meanwhile, has been responsible for some of the most unlistenable music ever made and, if you don't believe me, ask ex—label head David Geffen. He grew so frustrated with Young's peregrinations that he actually sued his own artist for deliberately making music that didn't sound like Neil Young, as though such a thing ever existed.

The man had already cut LPs as disparate as *Harvest*, *On the Beach*, *Rust Never Sleeps*, and *Re-ac-tor* before he even signed with Geffen; compared with that sequence, *Trans*, *Everybody's Rockin'*, and *Old Ways* were simply another day at the office.

Still, it is doubtful whether there is a single person on the planet, Neil Young included, who could hand-on-heart claim to have enjoyed every LP he's ever made, let alone agreed with every sentiment he's ever uttered. Admired, yes. Respected, for sure. Even grudgingly appreciated. But adored wholeheartedly for every record he's made? Ha.

Neil Young paid his first visit to the Hall of Fame in 1995, at the age of fifty. Disheveled mass mumbler Eddie Vedder introduced him onto the stage, in the same year that Vedder's own appalling Pearl Jam recorded the *Mirror Ball* album with Young: It wasn't an especially good record by any applicable standards. But the misstep wasn't Young's; it was Pearl Jam's. For who, beyond musicians who've worked with Young since dirt was young, could truly expect *not* to be led astray by the man? If the people who buy his records can't trust him, how can the people who make them?

From the introspection of *Tonight's the Night* to the fug of *Life*, and from the bombast of Crazy Horse to the down-home fiddles of the International Harvesters, Young has built his career upon shooting himself down. Forget all those other self-styled iconoclasts for whom the headlines bleed out with monotonous regularity—Young is the real thing.

Young was an angry old man in 1967, when he first arrived in Los Angeles from his native Canada, and he's an angry old man today, forty-plus years later. Still maintaining a more-or-less annual release schedule in an age when most of his peers (and successors) feel overworked if they put out more than three albums in a decade, Young has delivered albums through the mid- to late 2000s that contain some of the most searing sounds of his career, from the cataclysmic bathos of 2006's *Living With War* to the extended guitar jamborees that highlighted 2008's *Chrome Dreams II*. Plus, with "Let's Impeach the President," he set to popular music a refrain that many people were actually frightened to vocalize, for all the reasons set out in the song's third verse.

Forty years ago, you could barely turn around without tripping over someone else singing aloud his or her condemnation of the Vietnam War. In 1970, Young's commentary on the Kent State Massacre, where the National Guard shot and killed four students protesting the bombing of Cambodia, was recorded and chartbound before the headlines had even cooled.

Where is that dissent today? Where are the souls bared in musical opposition to the conflict in Iraq? Where are the angry young men of the 2000s—where are the voices raised and fists extended that could actually make Neil Young seem old? And can anyone even think of a word that rhymes with "Afghanistan"? In 1970, the occasional critic grumbled that George Harrison twinned "Bangladesh" with "such a mess," as though a better lyric might have solved the problem altogether. But at least he tried. Today, they take a quick flick through the thesaurus, then run off and write about something else.

The last time Neil toured with Crosby, Stills, and Nash, he named the outing the Freedom of Speech Tour, and played his *Living With War* album in its entirety every night.

When he stood up at the 2003 Hall of Fame, he likened America to "a giant gas-guzzling SUV" and claimed that its driver was "drunk as a fucking skunk." And he scored his biggest hit ever with an album of acoustic love songs, which is why his best records tend to be the louder, electric ones. Patti Smith once said that it's up to the young people to make the world better. But Neil Young is the only person who has consistently made the effort, and whether they live to a ripe old age or wind up dying in their prime, not one of rock's so-called bad boys (or girls) is worth a pint of Neil Young's piss when it comes to really standing up for what he believes in (whatever that might be).

CHAPTER FOURTEEN

Welcome Back My Friends to the Show That Seriously Goes on Forever, or, Don't Forget to Check Your Sell-By Date

In which you, the reader, ask, "If you don't like new music by new bands, then what about new music by old bands? Surely you must like that?" Well, since you asked so nicely, no. Especially when they had to re-form before making it.

WHEN LED ZEPPELIN REFORMED in December 2007, to play a concert in memory of the recently deceased Atlantic records chief Ahmet Ertegun, not an eyebrow was raised in questioning response.

More than any band since the Beatles, Zeppelin was *the* act that everybody wanted to see reunited. No matter that their drummer was dead, nor that two of the band, vocalist Robert Plant and guitarist

Jimmy Page, had already dedicated a couple of years in the mid-1990s to essentially recreating the Zeppelin legend as Page-Plant. They didn't do it under the Zeppelin name: Therefore, it wasn't Zeppelin.

It's like the current incarnation of the New York Dolls. When they originally formed in the mid-2000s, just three members of the original lineup were still alive. By the time they got around to releasing an album, only two were still with us—the same two (vocalist David Johansen and guitarist Sylvain Sylvain) who were playing together with equal style and substance back in the late 1970s. Now, why is it that nobody cared back then, but they're going apeshit for it now? Because back then, they were the David Johansen Band. Today they're the New York Dolls.

What a difference a name makes. Seriously. It really doesn't seem to matter what the actual makeup of a re-forming band might be. Just so long as their name is on the concert ticket, just so long as you can buy the souvenir poster and T-shirt and a little plastic wallet to keep you cell phone in, and then turn around to your friends and tell them, "I was there." I was there the night Christ returned to Earth. He encored with "Jet Boy." Or "Whole Lotta Love."

How much did it cost to witness the Second Coming of the Zep? A news item in the March 2008 issue of *Record Collector* magazine reported that the average price paid for tickets (face value £125) was £7,425 *each*—more than $10,000.

We single out Zeppelin because of the amount of money involved, and the heights of euphoria that their reunion provoked. But we could just as easily have settled upon any of the so many reunions that have blossomed across the music scene over the last fifteen years or so, a flowering that has brought so many of our old heroes back to life that looking at the summer concert schedule is like seeing your entire life pass before you. Or turning up for school one day and finding that all your teachers are in the desks alongside you.

There's Green Day touring the same circuit as the Sex Pistols

There's Blues Traveler at a festival with the Allman Brothers.

There's the Smashing Pumpkins (who themselves broke up and then re-formed, when they discovered that, *seriously, guys, nobody cares about your solo projects*) playing alongside the Who.

And there's the Who themselves, who should really be called the Two for the same reasons that the *Anthology*-era Beatles were jokingly renamed the Threetles, rattling around at the same time as the Jam, who at least had the decency to admit that, with one-third of their lineup absenting himself from the show, they ought to change their name a little. They became From the Jam, which isn't simply a better name—it's also a lot more honest.

A band name is also a brand name, a title people come to trust to deliver a certain sound, a certain style, and a certain type of song. To change any of those commodities is an artist's prerogative, of course, because you'll never get anywhere by standing still forever. Unless you're Status Quo, of course, but that's what they do, and we love them for it.

But would it be right for a group to continue trading under the old name, when the new sound is so totally removed from any that the audience might expect?

If you bought a Picasso and it looked like a Turner, you'd be perfectly within your rights to complain. If you bought some cornflakes and they tasted of washing-up powder, back to the store with the things.

But what if you bought a Journey record and it sounded like A Flock of Seagulls? We discussed this dilemma when we talked of Genesis and Yes, and were suitably shaken by our findings. When Jefferson Airplane realized that they really didn't want to make great records any longer, they changed their name to Jefferson Starship and tootled along making okay ones. Then, when that grew dull and it was time to *really* start scraping the musical barrel, they shortened their name even further, to Starship. Which meant, when twenty years of correspondingly diminishing returns were at an end, they could gather back much of the original crew and be reborn as Jefferson Airplane again.

That is how it ought to be done. They still weren't the *real* Airplane, of course. But they were closer in spirit than any previous incarnation, and at least they had distanced themselves from "We Built This City," a song that so succinctly sums up everything that was wrong with rock in the '80s that even Fleetwood Mac's "Big Love" sounds good alongside it.

Unfortunately, the Airplane were also an exception. Far more frequently, revivals will stick to the old name come hell or high water, no matter how badly warmed up the remnants are. With the emphasis sadly on the word *remnants*. The Sensational Alex Harvey Band reformed without Alex Harvey, and Thin Lizzy without Phil Lynott. People flooded to see them. Clearly, there are some villages missing their idiots tonight. Do people not care? Are they really happy just to get the band name in their "gigs I've seen" list and hear someone, *anyone*, play the old songs?

Or maybe they simply don't know any better. When Fleetwood Mac were forced off the road in 1975 by one personal calamity too many (and this was *before* Buckingham-Nicks arrived to inject their own version of *Peyton Place* into the proceedings), management was so incensed that it literally formed an entire new band and sent that out on the road in their stead. It was two weeks before the "real" Mac's lawsuits caught up with the tour, but did even one of the kids who waved pretzels in a dozen packed arenas notice that the beards had grown shorter, or the hair was somehow wavier? If they did, they kept it to themselves.

Likewise, when American promoters were offered a tour by an apparently re-formed Deep Purple in 1980, did any of them even think to ask which lineup of the band they were getting? The classic Gillan-Glover-led powerhouse? The more staid Coverdale-Hughes-fronted combo? A new combination of the two?

Or perhaps a bunch of refugees from the Steppenwolf revival, plus the guy who sang lead vocals on the band's first, forgotten, three albums?

Bingo!

Oh how we laughed as "Deep Purple" toured the land, leaving riot and refunds in their tacky wake. Oh how we chuckled when front man Rod Evans insisted, "There were several formations of the band, and it never seemed to really affect the fans of the music, as long as it was played up to a certain par. They just wanted to hear the music." And oh how we danced when the deception was finally stopped (again in the courts) and Purple could return to the grave in which they'd been sleeping since 1976.

Of course, they wouldn't stay buried for long, and four years later, the band returned, only this time with the classic lineup, and they've been rattling along ever since: a rare example of a reunion that convenes with good intentions and reestablishes itself as a true working unit. Maybe you wouldn't go see Deep Purple play in 2008 and expect it to be the same as when you caught them first in 1973. But you wouldn't feel so cheated, either, because the reunion has lasted almost twenty-five years, and they've erected a whole new career in that time.

When Led Zeppelin returned in 2007, they replaced their late drummer with his son; when Van Halen went out that same year, Eponymous Eddie hired his own boy to play bass. And when Boston reconvened in 2008, they were fronted by Tommy DeCarlo, a fan who posted his covers on his MySpace page and wound up in the band.

The Allmans came back in 1989, to discover a whole new audience growing up in the wake of the jam bands that now flooded the American college circuit. Lynyrd Skynyrd joined them there in 1991, nine years after first giving up the ghost (and fourteen years after the heart of the band was torn out by a plane disaster), to find that an entire *lifestyle* had grown up around their first album cover. Traffic jammed, Camel rode, Santana sorted out their differences. Artists whom you'd completely written off because they sucked so bad through the 1980s were bouncing back. And some of them seemed revitalized.

Maybe it was the sight of so many familiar faces. It must be cripplingly lonely at the top when all the bands that you grew up with

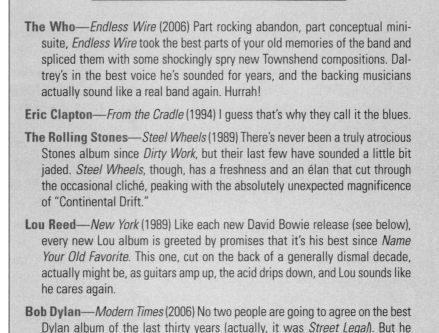

Thirty Years of Hurt: The Best New Music by Our Beloved Old Friends

The Who—*Endless Wire* (2006) Part rocking abandon, part conceptual mini-suite, *Endless Wire* took the best parts of your old memories of the band and spliced them with some shockingly spry new Townshend compositions. Daltrey's in the best voice he's sounded for years, and the backing musicians actually sound like a real band again. Hurrah!

Eric Clapton—*From the Cradle* (1994) I guess that's why they call it the blues.

The Rolling Stones—*Steel Wheels* (1989) There's never been a truly atrocious Stones album since *Dirty Work*, but their last few have sounded a little bit jaded. *Steel Wheels*, though, has a freshness and an élan that cut through the occasional cliché, peaking with the absolutely unexpected magnificence of "Continental Drift."

Lou Reed—*New York* (1989) Like each new David Bowie release (see below), every new Lou album is greeted by promises that it's his best since *Name Your Old Favorite*. This one, cut on the back of a generally dismal decade, actually might be, as guitars amp up, the acid drips down, and Lou sounds like he cares again.

Bob Dylan—*Modern Times* (2006) No two people are going to agree on the best Dylan album of the last thirty years (actually, it was *Street Legal*). But he

have broken down and died. Maybe it was the realization that you got past forty and yes, it was horrid, but you're now facing fifty and you're only middle-aged. You've got the rest of your life in front of you, so you'd better start having fun again. Or maybe it was simply relief that the '80s were over, because they really were as bad as we remember.

Even the Who returned. Several times. Technically, the Who ended with the *Who Are You* album and the death of drummer Keith Moon in 1978. In fact, they plugged on for two more albums, released remains one of the few people who, having scraped the bottom of the barrel in the '80s, has actually been getting better ever since.

Deep Purple—*Purpendicular* (1998) Six albums into their rebirth and Ritchie Blackmore walked out. In came Steve Morse and the new blood reawakened what had been growing an increasingly over-slick operation. It's not *In Rock*, but it's not *Slaves and Masters*, either.

Aerosmith—*Nine Lives* (1997) Yes, it's preposterous, yes, it's absurd, and yes, Aerosmith still sound like the smirking teenagers they were back in 1975. "Love Is Hard on the Knees," they sing. Oh, you wicked wags. But isn't that what you want from Aerosmith? Something to spend your day smirking at and wishing that you could feel this crass again? I bet Steve Tyler didn't spend two hours this morning wondering where he'd put the unpaid gas bill.

Jimmy Page & Robert Plant—*Walking Into Clarksdale* (1998) Not quite Zeppelin, but shockingly close enough.

Peter Gabriel—*Security* (1982) One of the few talents that sustained us through the very early 1980s, Gabriel proved that it was not hubris that persuaded him to walk out on Genesis, but a genuine need to explore exciting new sonic frontiers. Of course, he went down the pan soon enough (his next album, *So*, should be thrown to the pigs), but *Security* is a glorious clatter of malice, mood, and momentum.

David Bowie—*Hours* (1999) His dark days lasted so long that it seemed he would never get back on track. But this gorgeous collection of love-and-loss songs remains such a potent examination of looming middle age that the old boy actually sounds young again.

over the next five years, as though doggedly determined to prove that they were not dependent on the drummer for the magic spark. But when was the last time you or anybody else you know woke up craving a quick spin of *Face Dances* or *It's Hard*? Or *Join Together*, the soggy souvenir box set documenting their 1989 reunion bash? Yes, "Eminence Front" may have come on the radio and caught you singing the Doobies' "Long Train Running" before you realized it's not the same song, but that's about as good as it got.

CHAPTER FIFTEEN

Charity Begins at Someone Else's Home, or, One More Push, and I Think We'll Break the Ethiopian Market Wide Open

In which we consider the gentle art of giving, and ask who shall pass first into the kingdom of heaven: the poor man who has nothing, but who happily gives away what he can? Or the rich fucker who gets guilted into playing a twenty-minute gig by Bob Geldof?

BONO STANDS UPON THE STAGE, his eyes sharp, his voice steady. Behind him, his bandmates slow the music to a rhythmic throb. "Every time I clap my hands," Bono says slowly, "another person dies of hunger."

He starts to clap. One. Two. Three. The silence in the hall is absolute. Four. Five. Six. The audience scarcely dares breathe. Seven.

Eight. Nine. Every time he claps his hands, another person dies of hunger.

And then a voice rings out from the back of the room: "Well, you'd better stop fucking clapping then."

Bono is one of rock's great humanitarians. Even in the '80s, when the global reach of rock 'n' roll was so much smaller (the Iron and Bamboo Curtains were able to deaden its voice to millions), Bono spoke to the conscience of the world.

He spoke of racism. "I always say there are two Americas. There's one that's spelt Amerika and that's eight channels, that's Ronald Reagan, that's pistols and the Ku Klux Klan. But I'm interested in America, which is open space and a newfound land."

He spoke of intolerance. "I was in the middle of 'Sunday Bloody Sunday' and there was a party of people giving it the 'eff the British' line. I stopped the show and said, 'Okay, it's all over. You're completely misreading the group.'"

He spoke of injustice. "You can fall asleep in the comfort of your freedoms. We can't right all wrongs, but we can find people who can help to do it."

He spoke of unity. "[Ireland] has been cut in two for too long. You can see the scars on people's lives."

He spoke of togetherness. "John Lennon [said] of Pete Best, 'He's not a Beatle.' We're all Beatles."

In fact, as the years mounted up and the press cuttings with them, there wasn't much that he didn't speak of. Maybe by choice, maybe because every time another television producer had a show coming up that needed a rock 'n' roll perspective included, they'd call up Bono and ask him what he thought. And Bono would tell them. Calmly, straightforwardly, sensitively.

"You only get disillusioned if you had illusions to begin with." Wow. I mean, phew. I mean, is this dude perceptive or what?

There's a great moment in the Band Aid record, at the end of the second verse. If you don't remember the original record, there was a host of the day's top popsters, very few of whom you would actually recognize today ("Look, Ma, it's Paul Young! And there, it's Bananarama!! And isn't that *Duran Duran?*"), each singing a line or two of what was truly the first modern Christmas carol. They all take their turn, the Boy Georges and George Michaels, the Paul Wellers and Stings, and then it's Bono's chance to shine. And what line does he get? What line did lyricist Bob Geldof probably stay up all night cackling over, just *knowing* who he was going to stick it to?

"The Christmas bells that ring there are the clanging chimes of doom. Well, tonight thank God it's them instead of you."

Here, Bono, here's your line. And Bono? He sang it like a songbird. Two lines, and he slammed more emotion, more heart, more from-the-bottom-of-my-soulfulness into them than the rest of the party packed into the remainder of the song.

Because that is what Bono does. He makes you believe him. You believe him when he tells you he's his own worst enemy, you believe him when he tells you he might make a good president and, most of all, you believe him when he tells you that his clap can kill.

One. Two. Three.

So why does he strike so many people as such a sanctimonious little twerp?

U2 formed in 1977 within the first wave of would-be musicians who, inspired by the example of their own idols, saw rock 'n' roll as a career choice, as opposed to something you did while you were still young enough to do it, before real life charged in and sent you down a coal mine.

Unlike many of the bands springing to life in that year, however, they never pledged allegiance to punk rock. From the outset (or at least as close to the outset as their earliest available recordings will allow), they pursued a more anthemic brand of music, somewhere in between fellow Irishmen Thin Lizzy and "You'll Never Walk Alone." It was a fascinating hybrid at the time, and the band's early recordings—albums in 1980 (*Boy*), 1981 (*October*) and 1983 (*War*)—resonated with a spirited incredulity that really did sound impressive. Guitarist The Edge had a sound all his own, the rhythm section was as solid as the ground beneath your feet, and Bono had this catch-in-the-voice thing that he did with the lyrics that almost made you weep alongside him. You could *feel* his pain. You could *touch* his suffering. You could *hear* those chimes of doom. And you *knew* that the world would be a better place if we all just listened to Bono.

You cannot criticize the man. He has his beliefs and he adheres to them like glue. Better than glue, in fact, because you can't wash Bono off. When he gives his all to a cause, he stays given. Thank God there's so much of him to go around.

Not physically. In the early days of U2's ascent, around the time the band was so famously filmed conquering the slopes of Colorado's Red Rocks amphitheater, a rival British performer compared him to a pudgy little mountain goat, scampering around on the hillside. But that's not what I mean. Spiritually. The man's heart is just so huge, there's a place in it for everyone. A bit like God's, really, and there are corners of the world, once-neglected little enclaves on the brink of man-made extinction, where maybe they already venerate Bono for focusing the light of the world on their plight and making their lives so much better.

Imagine. Like the cargo cults that once proliferated in the Pacific Ocean, where superstitious natives venerated the odds and sods that passing aircraft accidentally dropped on their heads, there could be tribes of naked natives wandering around in blue Fly shades that they've carved from coconuts, saluting one another with their arms bent above their heads like the boy on the cover of the first U2 album. Except you know they all have iPods and cell phones now, and the only corners of the planet that are truly untouched are the ones that Bono *hasn't* talked about, because nobody knows they exist. The moment we make first contact, they're going to be glugging Coke and moping to emo and downloading bad Internet porn, just like the rest of us. Civilization—don'tcha just love it?

A joke: Bono, Sting, and the singer from Midnight Oil walk into a bar.

"What can I get you, gentlemen?" asks the barman.

"I'll have whatever he's having," say Bono, nodding toward the singer from Midnight Oil. "I'll have whatever he's having," say the singer from Midnight Oil, nodding toward Sting. "And I'll have whatever *he's* having," says Sting, nodding back toward Bono.

So the barman stands there for a moment, while the trio look on expectantly, and then the door bursts open and in walks Bob Geldof. "And I suppose *you* want the same as them, don't you?" asks the barman, but Geldof shakes his head angrily. "What, you mean to say they've already decided without me?"

In the world of rock 'n' roll royalty, Bob Geldof is the grand poobah of pop. Other stars may be more famous, others may be more glamorous. Others might even shave and comb their hair more often. But when it comes to getting things done—and not only that, but making sure that they *stay* done—Bob Geldof has no equal.

It wasn't always like this. A former journalist, the Irish correspondent for one of the London music papers, Geldof brought his band the Boomtown Rats to prominence in the early punk era, before they spiraled stylistically off in other directions and essentially blueprinted what would become the New Wave. By the time of their biggest hit, "I Don't Like Mondays," a commentary on the first major American school shooting, the Rats were arguably the biggest, and certainly the most creative, of all the groups operating within that particular sphere, another of those rare beams of sunshine that suggested that maybe the '80s wouldn't be so bad after all.

But they'd peaked, and now they started to fade. Which is when Geldof discovered the famine in Ethiopia. Or, more accurately, he discovered a BBC news report on the famine in Ethiopia, but the end result was much the same. Sensibly sickened by the broadcast scenes of suffering, he began phoning up his celebrity friends and demanding that something be done. And they agreed.

This is not the place to wonder what might have happened had they not, had they just asked him if he knew what time it was (the

145

news broadcast went out well after ten at night; one would imagine that most of the people he called were asleep) and hung up. Or, once he'd got a few on board, what kind of pressures he might have been able to exert to make sure that everyone else joined in.

But the legendary '80s puppet show *Spitting Image* aired a tremendous parody of the resultant all-star gathering, via a song called "We're Scared of Bob": "We're scared of Bob, we're scared of Geldof / We're scared that if we try to turn him down, we'll all get killed off." Or at least outed in the tabloid press of the day, which probably amounted to the same thing. LET THEM STARVE! SAYS POP STAR ****** THEY PROBABLY DON'T BUY MY RECORDS ANYWAY.

A quarter of a century on, events such as Band Aid (the record) and Live Aid (the concert) really don't seem too remarkable. The intervening years have seen so many charitable concerns pluck a few guitar strings in order to loosen our purse strings that it sometimes seems incredible if a calamity, disaster, or government-sponsored fuckup (Katrina) *isn't* immediately answered by an all-star something-or-other.

At the time, however, although it wasn't quite unique, Band Aid was certainly unparalleled. It is true that through the late 1960s, the Civil War that ravaged the breakaway Nigerian state of Biafra was the subject of a number of rock 'n' roll benefits, but they were small potatoes, even if stars the stature of Joan Baez and Jimi Hendrix did turn out to support them.

A few years later, in 1971, George Harrison mobilized the somewhat grander Concert for Bangladesh to raise funds and awareness for the recently flood-flattened Asian nation. With musical contributions from fellow Beatle Ringo, Eric Clapton, Bob Dylan, Ravi Shankar, and more (*really?* Who else was possibly left?), two performances at Madison Square Garden raised a then-staggering $243,000 for the cause—and then got completely bound up in red tape when it was discovered that they'd forgotten to apply for tax-exempt status, and Uncle Sam wanted his share to take away and spend on bombs. The

Ten Singles Raising Money for Good Causes . . . but Can We Just Give Them the Money and Not Hear the Record, Please?

"That's What Friends Are For"—Dionne Warwick, Stevie Wonder, Gladys Knight, and Elton John (1985—American Foundation for AIDS Research)

"Heroes"—Suzi Quatro, Bronski Beat, Wendy Roberts (1986—Children in Need)

"Everybody Wants to Run the World"—Tears for Fears (1986—Sport Aid)

"Ferry 'Cross the Mersey"—Paul McCartney, Holly Johnson, the Christians, Gerry Marsden (1989—Hillsborough Stadium disaster)

"You've Got a Friend"—Big Fun & Sonia (1990—Childline)

"Love Can Build a Bridge"—Cher, Chrissie Hynde, Eric Clapton, Neneh Cherry (1995—Comic Relief)

"Knocking on Heaven's Door"—Ted Christopher (1996—Dunblane massacre)

"What's Going On"—Artists Against AIDS (2001—AIDS relief and 9/11 . . . a peculiar combination, but no matter)

"Grief Never Grows Old"—One World Project (2004 Asian tsunami relief)

"Do They Know It's Halloween"—North American Halloween Prevention Initiative (2005—UNICEF)

Vietnam War was still going badly; it was about time these damned peacenik hippies paid their fair share toward it.

Because, sad though it is to recall, that was how "polite society" viewed the Concert for Bangladesh. It was Beatle George, back on the same subcontinental hobby horse that he'd been riding ever since he met that wacky maharishi character, and a bunch of his long-haired smelly cronies trying to prove that they weren't all as bad as they were painted. "Well, Mr. Unwashed Pop Star, let me tell you this. Your bleeding-heart liberal pinko commie comrades might think you're the hot patootie. But *I* know you're still a draft-dodging sack of shit, so stick *that* in your bong and smoke it."

Or words to that effect.

As a humanitarian gesture, Bangladesh was beautiful. As a countercultural peace offering to a society that still regarded rock 'n' rollers as barely a step or two above pubic lice, it was about as impressive as Tiffany's next comeback, and the business with the tax man only confirmed its total absurdity. Goddammit, if they couldn't remember to sort *that* out, how the hell are they going to solve the rest of the world's problems?

In 1981, Princess Diana became the first "commoner" to be allowed official entry into the traditionally closed circles of the British royal family, when she married the heir to the throne. And from the get-go, she captivated the world with her youth, vitality, beauty, and humor.

She was hip as hell. Whereas her husband, Prince Charles, once acknowledged a mild taste for the Three Degrees, a soulful trio of female vocalists who enjoyed a handful of hits in the mid-1970s, Diana threw herself wholeheartedly into the 1980s pop scene.

She danced to Duran Duran, and she knew which one was Roger.

She could sing along to Wham!

She may even have had a Howard Jones poster on her wall.

She was a trendsetter, she was groovy, she was with it. She was even friends with Elton John, which is why it is so *shameful* that, when she died, the best he could muster as a tribute to her memory was a shoddy retread of a song that he wrote for Marilyn Monroe, as though there were any parallels whatsoever to be drawn between Saint Diana and an adulterous, drug-addicted blond nymphomaniac.

Diana legitimized pop music in the eyes of the establishment. True, a few of the older media guard raised their eyebrows in despair when she was snapped a-bopping and a-hopping into the wee small hours to the strains of Simon Smith & His Amazing Dancing Durannies. But they indulged her because she was young, and her youth became contagious. Soon, everyone was a-bopping and a-hopping, and the only cloud on the horizon was—well, rock 'n' roll is all very nice, but what is it actually *good* for?

It is good for the world! With one mighty leap (or, at least, a long night making phone calls), Bob Geldof mobilized the greatest army of pop stars ever seen in one place, all singing their hearts out to raise money for the hungry. Neither did it end there. Six weeks later, the same exercise was repeated in America, as USA for Africa made a similar, Geldof-led gesture.

Live Aid was next, a global concert with near-simultaneous shows taking place in cities all over the planet, but centered in London and Philadelphia. The first time Geldof told copromoter Harvey Goldsmith he wanted fifty bands, the promoter joked, "There aren't fifty bands on the whole planet." In fact, they ended up with close to a hundred.

Not everything went smoothly, of course. Bob Dylan raised Geldof's hackles by suggesting that "it would be nice if some of this money went to the American farmers." A few performers (the Rats, Paul McCartney) lost their vocal mics in the midst of their performances, and a few more lost a lot of respect because of what they performed—it gets tiresome beating on Bowie and the Stones for making such bad records as the '80s went on, but we would be so remiss not to mention Mick and David's "Dancing in the Street," a performance of such distasteful period excess that, when they promised that it would never be heard again once Live Aid was over, even the bootleggers raised a cheer. How cruel, therefore, for them to renege on their word and release it as a single just a few weeks later. They claimed their hand was swayed by Public Demand. Me, I reckon they just lost a bet.

Chilling, too, was that moment when, during one technical hitch or another, the Cars' superlatively abysmal "Drive" was broadcast, accompanied by raw footage from the famine zone. Donations spiked so high for those few minutes that it's a wonder they didn't just cancel the rest of the concert and play more somber music instead.

Perhaps the oddest performance of all, though, was delivered by Joan Baez, a veteran of so many past benefits, causes, and wrongs-needing-righting that it was surprising she hadn't thought of Live Aid herself. Instead, she smiled munificently out upon the crowd and greeted "you children of the '80s" with the words, "This is your Woodstock, and it's long overdue."

What a peculiar thing to say. Forget the obvious difference that one went on for three days in a muddy field in the back end of nowhere, while the other was staged in a couple of sports arenas in the hearts of two of the most populous cities in the west: Woodstock was the intended signal for a countercultural revolution; Live Aid was a technological money machine. Woodstock was designed to free peoples' consciousness; Live Aid was intended to move their check-writing hand.

Live Aid was a cash cow plain and simple and, no matter how noble the intentions behind it, Starvin' Marvin was never intended to be the sole beneficiary of so much largesse. From the newest kids on the rock 'n' rolling block to the legendary megaliths that re-formed for the occasion (both Black Sabbath and Led Zeppelin convened one-off reunions), the only reason these bands hauled themselves out of bed on a Saturday to take their places on the conveyor belt and await their day in the sun was because they were guaranteed more exposure in their twenty Live Aid minutes than from every other concert they'd played in their lives combined.

And, if you don't believe that, think on this: The following week, every artist who appeared at Live Aid experienced a significant jump in their catalog sales, while almost every one with a single on the UK chart saw it go up a few places. All, that is, apart from poor Adam Ant, who actually performed his new single instead of sticking with the hits. He went *down* the chart.

What was it Chumbawamba called their first LP? *Pictures of Starving Children Sell Records.*

Of course, it is futile to sit here and pick holes in Live Aid. Yes, it gave Geldof a whole new career as a philanthropist, when his life as a successful musician seemed over. But so what? How can you place one man's inadvertent self-aggrandizement against the well-being of millions? Live Aid did what it was intended to. It raised money for the charity, which spent it on food that was fed to the hungry, and a country was saved.

But we also lost something that day. We lost the very last vestiges of the outlaw mystique that had always given rock 'n' roll that secretive gleam in its eye.

Once, the media mainstream laughed at the presumptiveness of pop stars daring to speak out on the big issues of the day; when draft-dodging rockers bitched about conscription, when pill-popping wastrels demanded the legalization of pot, when long-haired sex maniacs demanded free contraception for all.

Now, it couldn't get enough of them and, suddenly, it seemed as though everybody had a cause to espouse, or a few words to say about somebody else's. Barely two months after Live Aid, the first Farm Aid benefit sprang up, quite possibly out of Bob Dylan's closing bitterness. Less than a year later, Amnesty International's Conspiracy of Hope concert tour traveled the world in aid of human rights, and was followed in 1988 by the similarly far-reaching Human Rights Now! outing.

Artists United Against Apartheid targeted the then-incumbent South African government (a point also taken by the Free Nelson Mandela campaign). The Beastie Boys' Free Tibet concerts in the mid- to late 1990s focused attention upon China's occupation of that country; the Concert for Peace 2000 networked two thousand concerts worldwide into one massive benefit for the reconstruction of Kosovo.

But how many of them do we remember today? How many did we even notice before disaster fatigue finally kicked in and every one blurred into another? Try to remember today the litany of lamentations that the rich and the powerful sent up through the '80s and into the early '90s. Even the music is forgotten.

But the griefcore kept on rolling, to reach its peak in 1992 at a concert staged to remember the recently deceased Freddie Mercury, and to raise funds to help fight the disease that killed him.

Mercury's death stunned observers. Not the world; vast swaths of it had never even heard of the man, as I discovered while freelancing at the *Seattle Times*, and asking the relevant editor if I could write the obituary. "Who's Freddie Mercury?" he asked. Among the people who had heard of him, however, who had spent the last eighteen years being alternately entertained, outraged, and sometimes plain nonplussed by Queen's antics, the death came completely out of the blue.

Nobody outside of his own immediate circle even knew Mercury was ill when, on November 22, 1991, it was announced that he was suffering from AIDS. The following day he was dead and, over the next four months, bandmates Roger Taylor, Brian May, and John Deacon worked to put together a tribute concert that would double as a benefit for AIDS research. AIDS Aid, although they had the taste and decency to eschew that particular title.

Like so many of the mega-charity festivals that preceded it, the Mercury concert boasted an eccentric bill, one that highlighted only a handful of the names that one would automatically associate (or otherwise!) with Queen, but which bristled with amusement regardless. Def Leppard were there, Guns N' Roses, Metallica, Robert Plant, Extreme, Seal, Elton John and George Michael, and David Bowie, who ran through a nifty triptych of hits and then, as a hundred thousand people did whatever they do at those festival gigs where the stage is a pinprick behind a few pillars, he broke away from the songbook and spoke slowly, calmly, but assuredly emotionally, about the ravages of "this relentless disease." Then he fell to his knees and, eyes closed now, he recited the Lord's Prayer.

What a fucking prat.

"In hindsight, as it was so alien a gesture in the context of rock, it remains a favorite personal rock 'moment' for me," Bowie said a decade later. "It was astounding to find that I could complete the prayer in front of so many thousands of people, without hearing a pin drop."

Astounding? Maybe so. But it was also disturbing, as though you and all the other millions watching on TV were imposing upon one man's private grief; even in the privacy of your own front room, shifting awkwardly in your seat, waiting for the humiliation to end (*For fuck's sake, Bowie, my parents are watching this!*), and absolutely transfixed by the sheer grotesque theater of it all.

We were all familiar with the tabloid television trick of rushing up to the survivors of major disasters and asking them how they were feeling, while the camera lens tracked their every tear. *How do you think I feel*, they replied. *He was a miserable old git and I'm glad he's gone*. But this was different. This wasn't the cameras searching for tears: This was the tears in search of the cameras and then, having found them, pinning them to the wall.

It was a process that more recent years have rendered so routine that many rolling news services actively solicit personal film footage from the victims of disasters, while combing the streets in search of the very same people who comb the streets looking for them. In 1992, however, it was untapped soil, and some people *still* can't watch the Freddie-Aid DVD for fear of it sneaking up on them again.

Himself undoubtedly aware that people were rapidly tiring of being asked to dig deep, both financially and emotionally, for this cause and for that, Geldof presented a second spectacular, 2005's Live 8, which set out to end world poverty by not actually asking its viewers (or its participants) for money, hoping to pressure the political establishment to make the commitment instead.

Live 8 was staged on the twentieth anniversary of Live Aid, and most memorable for persuading Pink Floyd to reform. Any success that the concert might have achieved has yet to manifest itself in any material terms; rather, the food riots that struck Haiti, Indonesia, and parts of Africa in early 2008 would suggest that things have only gotten worse since then, not better. But it was a nice thought.

However, the festival that best sums up the entire sorry charade of the modern rock charity, and places everything in the harshest, teeth-grinding perspective, is politician Al Gore's Live Earth, in 2007.

Across a dozen sold-out venues worldwide, 125 bands, plus count-
less presenters, roadies, caterers, merchants, broadcasters, and "I'm
with the band"ers, were flown and driven to their date with destiny,
together with however many tens of thousands of people could be
crammed in to watch them, and however many more were required
from a logistical standpoint. Somebody had to sell all those veggie
burgers.

And somebody, one hopes, is still planting all the trees required to
offset the ecological carnage that the carnival wrought. The watchdog
website CarbonFootprint.com later estimated that Live Earth's total
environmental cost was the equivalent of three thousand normal people going about their business for a full year. Nice one, Al. Good to
know you *really* thought that one through. Next time, why don't you
just hold the show on a polar ice cap. Let's give that ozone hole something serious to think about.

The strange thing is, kids—and yes, let's be patronizing enough to
assume that the majority of people who spend the most time listening to and paying attention to the messages contained in their pop
music are kids—*do* want to change the world.

They *do* want to take responsibility for the future of the planet,
they *do* want to grow up in a better, healthier, safer world, and they
don't want to inherit the pox-ridden, war-weary, gas-guzzling mess
that the last generation have created.

But they'd want it *regardless* of what they are told by the old men
in charge, and regardless of how many times Bono claps his hands.
They want it because every generation wants it, from the long-haired
cold-war radicals whose consciences led them into the protest movement of the early 1960s, to the even longer-haired hippie hordes who
literally put their freedom on the line to protest the Vietnam War, and
on to the contrarily short-haired punks who first took on social injustice in the UK.

That was the difference. Prior to Live Aid, when politics met rock
'n' roll the collision was ugly. It was the sound of rifle-wielding
National Guardsmen wading into a crowd of half-stoned longhairs

singing "Feel Like I'm Fixing to Die Rag," or firing live ammo into a group of protesting students. It was the sound of London riot police beating a tattoo with batons on their shields as they bear down on kids protesting the racist firebombing of a Bengali family. It was the rumble of tanks in the street where you live, and the clang of the jail doors behind you. It was real.

Post—Live Aid, it was *still* real. People were still starving, dying, being locked away for their personal beliefs, or chained and beaten for their sexual preferences. But it somehow seems a lot less frightening when another third-rate pop star stands up to do a Geldof, and uses the exact same tone of voice that NBC have hooked to their "coming soon" trailers: *Next week, a tribute to the Ruritanian earthquake disaster that you are not going to want to miss.*

Once, a tragedy demanded direct action. Today, it is apparently enough to sing a song about it, as though there is nothing so horrific, so mind-bendingly, gut-wrenchingly, heart-stoppingly terrible that it cannot be remedied by gathering together a handful of past-their-sell-by-date pop stars and having them warble a few lines of solace.

And every time *I* clap my hands, another sanctimonious rock 'n' roll martyr dies of shame.

One. Two. Three. Four. Six hundred seventy-five. Six hundred seventy-six. Six hundred seventy-seven.

Don't worry—I can keep this up all night.

CHAPTER SIXTEEN

A Glimmer of Hope,
or,
Let It Rut

In which, in response to the last few chapters' dire catalogs of calumny and suffering, we discover that there is one band who have bucked every trend that this book has mourned over, who did stand tall while every other act sucked dirt, and who never, ever let the Man forget who's really boss. It's just a shame that they didn't exist.

THEY CAME FROM THE SOUTH, but were they laid-back? Were they soothing? Were they . . . the *Marshall Tucker Band*? Hell, no! They were Black Oak Arkansas, and they were the biggest, baddest, meanest noise on God's own Earth, run out of their hometown at an early age and sent to live in the hills for crimes against propriety, stealing instruments for a living, and playing high on the hog, and then gigging and gigging right up until they burst onto their homeland's startled consciousness like pimples on prom night.

They were rash and brash, they were big and bouncy, and Jim Dandy flaunted himself without shame. The cut of his trousers

157

revealed the cut of his manhood and, just in case you didn't look at it, he'd start thrashing his groin with a tambourine and humping the washboard that accompanied him through every other song.

When journalists wrote that Dandy sounded *black*, they didn't mean it as a compliment. Black Oak may well have been country boys at heart, but they were evil. But not evil in a "two pints of pentacles and a packet of virgins" kind of way. They were far worse than that. Most rock bands came to town and you had to lock up your daughters. A handful came to town and you'd lock up your sons as well. When Black Oak came to town, your lawn died, your cow stopped producing milk, and your Eagles records all spontaneously warped.

But the little girls understood, and so did the little boys. Which is why if Black Oak Arkansas had never existed somebody would have had to invent them; and why, once they folded in 1980, they were promptly reinvented. Welcome to the world of Spinal Tap, a band who have absolutely nothing to do with Black Oak Arkansas, but who remain the only group whose legend can live up to Black Oak's reality.

The longest running joke in rock 'n' roll, and the longest-running in-joke as well, *Spinal Tap* started life as a movie and became an institution; it was conceived as parody and was transformed into reality. It set out to puncture egos and wound up feeding them.

Two decades after Nigel Tufnel (former *National Lampoon* musical director Christopher Guest), Derek Smalls (writer/comedian Harry Shearer), and David St. Hubbins (*Laverne & Shirley* star Michael McKean) exploded out of celluloid and into the mass rock consciousness; two decades, too, after former Sparks drummer—turned-journalist John Mendelssohn first described their exploits as "a self-indulgent bore," Spinal Tap remain the legendary benchmark by which any number of rockers measure their own capacity for outrageousness.

Black Sabbath, Judas Priest, and Status Quo are all reliably pushed forward as originators of one Spinal Tappism or another, with Ian Gillan, whose own time with Sabbath coincided with that band's ill-judged attempt to tour a replica model of Stonehenge, proudly recalling, "We were rehearsing and [someone] said, 'Does anybody have any ideas for a stage set?' and Geezer [Butler] said, 'Stonehenge. Life-size, of course.'

"So [we] built an exact replica of Stonehenge, which is huge. No one gave it any thought, but we could only get it into two of the halls and even then it was only three of these things. The rest of them are in containers in a dock somewhere and they have been [ever since]." At the time, he dismissed the entire affair as one more silly interlude in the life of a heavy metal band. Today, *This Is Spinal Tap* has established it as one of his favorite anecdotes.

There were other, similar, recommendations. Spinal Tap have credited acts as disparate as Uriah Heep, Tom Petty, the Grateful Dead, and the insanely stupid bassist with an unnamed mid-'70s English rock band as offering them up further prototypes, while Aerosmith's Brad Whitford recalled, "The first time Steven [Tyler] saw it he didn't see any humor in it. That's how close to home it was. He was pissed! He was like, 'That's not funny!'"

The premise of *This Is Spinal Tap* is simple. The early-'80s expansion of the MTV universe had witnessed a growing fad for "rockumentaries": story-of-the-band-style biopics that allowed past members to air their grievances, ex-groupies to relate their experiences (but only the PG ones; anything involving three dwarves, a lungfish, and a zucchini the size of Connecticut would remain securely in the vault), and the band itself to speak at length about the need to put on a show for the people, give the kids a good time, and rock 'n' roll it all the way home.

But cowriter Guest denied that *This Is Spinal Tap* ever set out to mock its subjects. They were more than capable of doing that on their own, and, though it is a digression, let us pause for a moment to recall Pat Benatar's clod-hopping cover of Kate Bush's "Wuthering Heights." No matter what your opinion of Bush, conceited fawn or postmodern geniusette, you cannot deny that she cloaks her music with a certain ethereal pixie-dust allure. Benatar, on the other hand, cloaks hers in stiletto heels and a donkey jacket. How could you even *begin* to tell a joke at her expense?

𝕿𝖊𝖓 𝕸𝖔𝖗𝖊 𝕲𝖗𝖊𝖆𝖙 𝕽𝖔𝖈𝖐 𝕸𝖔𝖛𝖎𝖊𝖘 (with plots)

Stardust—David Essex, Adam Faith, Keith Moon, Dave Edmunds
All You Need Is Cash—Neil Innes, Eric Idle
Rock 'n' roll High School—the Ramones
Privilege—Paul Jones
200 Motels—Mothers of Invention
Help!—the Beatles
Slade in Flame—Slade
Performance—Mick Jagger, Edward Fox
Quadrophenia—Phil Daniels, Toyah Wilcox
Renaldo & Clara—Bob Dylan, Joan Baez

and 𝕿𝖊𝖓 𝖂𝖎𝖙𝖍𝖔𝖚𝖙

The Kids Are Alright—the Who
Cocksucker Blues—the Rolling Stones
Jimi—Jimi Hendrix
Don't Look Back—Bob Dylan
Ziggy Stardust: The Motion Picture—David Bowie
Glastonbury Fayre—Arthur Brown, Traffic, etc.
Rust Never Sleeps—Neil Young
One Plus One—Rolling Stones
Born to Boogie—T. Rex
Renaldo & Clara—Bob Dylan, Joan Baez

What Guest did care about was "the notion that people can become so obsessed by their world that they lose sense and awareness of how they appear to other people. They're so earnest about it." Neither was he targeting specific bands or individuals, despite what those same specific bands and individuals might like to think. Leave rock parody to the likes of Weird Al Yankovich, Julian Lennon, and Oasis, or *National Lampoon* if you want to hear it done well—their "Magical Misery Tour" is such spot-on-John that it isn't even funny.

From the moment *This Is Spinal Tap* debuted in the cinemas, and the first stirrings of what is now an immense cult began to make themselves felt, it was clear that Spinal Tap was no ordinary imaginary rock group. Or rather, it was, except the imagination had now stepped into reality.

The group's first release in any dimension that the average reader might have access to (i.e., this one) followed the release of the movie, in the form of a sound track album, and after all that earlier chatter about the band's imaginary American hits, it became a real one, climbing to number 121 in April 1984.

An astonishingly successful tour and a clutch of television appearances followed, ostensibly to promote the movie, but also to encourage the fomenting belief that Spinal Tap really did exist, which is where this entire saga becomes especially interesting.

We've all heard, for example, of the sad-sack bored housewives who sit and watch their afternoon soaps, and then fall in love with/travel to meet/decide to murder (etc.) one of the characters (hey, there's even a movie about it, Renée Zellweger's *Nurse Betty*. Watch it). Now, all of a sudden, we were reading about kids who saw the film, bought the sound track, caught the band on *Saturday Night Live*, and suddenly, you could stick your Twisted Sister and your Springsteens and all, 'cos I've got Spinal Tap on my wall.

December 1984 brought Spinal Tap's first single, an airing for the festively themed "Christmas With the Devil" (first heard on the *Saturday Night Live* performance), after which the group seemed to fade somewhat, their magnificence swamped by the coterie of bands that, strangely, seemed to be taking the Tap ethos to even more absurd extremes. Ratt come to mind for some peculiar reason. So do Mötley Crüe and Poison.

Spinal Tap returned in 1992 with a new album, *Break Like the Wind* (a *real* album this time, not imaginary ones like those that predated the movie), and a massive US/European tour ahead of them. Again the musicians slipped into full costume and full character; between touring, interviews, and meeting with fans, they spent more time that year in their Spinal Tap roles than they did actually being themselves, a feat of theatrical stamina that still boggles the mind.

Interest in the band went through the roof. Claiming they had all but broken up following the Japanese tour seen at the end of *This Is Spinal Tap*, Spinal Tap were drawn back together by the sheer adoration of their audience. Indeed, if one reads the metal press of the age, it was true. The early adoration of a misguided handful of true believers (as in, truly believing the whole thing was not a spoof) had swollen into a veritable army of fans for whom *This Is Spinal Tap* was as much a part of the heavy metal landscape as *Paranoid*, *Led Zeppelin IV*, and Budgie's *Never Turn Your Back on a Friend*.

Featuring guest appearances by Joe Satriani, Slash, Cher, Nigel look-alike Jeff Beck, Dweezil Zappa, and Steve Lukather (who coproduced the album), *Break Like the Wind* reached number sixty-one on the *Billboard* chart. A brace of singles, "Bitch School" and "Majesty of Rock," appeared in a clutch of limited, collectible editions; the tour emerged one of the most successful concert experiences of the year; and Spinal Tap even recorded a special version of the Christmas carol "We Three Kings" for inclusion on a charity CD. The entire rebirth was then preserved on VHS, via the *Return of Spinal Tap* concert movie.

The group's reemergence was not wholly altruistic. Christopher Guest later revealed that, under the terms of the band's contract with the company that now owned the rights to *This Is Spinal Tap*, the three actors were required to exercise their claim on their characters every couple of years to keep the arrangement from lapsing—just like a real band that has to make a new album every so often, in order to keep *their* contract alive.

Nineteen ninety-four brought CD-ROM and laser disc versions of the original film; 1996 saw the group surface once again, to cut a track for an IBM commercial. Nineteen ninety-eight brought the film's DVD debut; 2000 saw it back out again, and on every occasion, media interest shot through the roof. VH1's *The List*, *The Late Show With David Letterman*, and *The Daily Show With John Stewart* all invited the band into their studios in 2000; a new single, "Back From the Dead," appeared as an MP3 download, while a clutch of live shows took the band to such legendary landmarks as the Greek Theater in L.A. and Carnegie Hall in New York, where none other than Elvis Costello got up to guest with them.

Even more bizarre, the opening act on that outing was McKean, Guest, and Shearer again, appearing as their protest folk parody band the Folksmen, a subterfuge that was going down like the proverbial lead balloon before the whisper finally began inching around the theaters that one guy looked a lot like Derek Smalls . . . yeah, and the other one could be Nigel Tufnel's brother. And isn't that David St. Hubbins in an old man's balding wig? By the end of the Folksmens' set, the audience would be howling their approval, and howling even louder as the trio returned to the stage, one wig-change later, to start "Stinkin' Up the Great Outdoors," to take them down the "Sex Farm" and sing the praises of "Big Bottom"s.

This Is Spinal Tap remains the team's greatest triumph. Entertaining though it was, the Folksmen's movie outing, *A Mighty Wind*, never caught the public imagination as sharply as its predecessor, but how, in all honesty, could it? Without Nigel wrestling with a recalcitrant sandwich, without Derek trapped inside a sci-fi pod, without David looking on in horror as an eighteen-inch Stonehenge is dwarfed by dancing leprechauns, what movie could shoulder Spinal Tap out of the realms of legend?

Besides, *This Is Spinal Tap* had one thing that had barely been invented when *A Mighty Wind*'s protagonists were first blowing in the wind. It had Dobly.

CHAPTER SEVENTEEN

Welcome to the Machine, or, Thank Christ for the Bomb

In which we reach the end of our journey and are overcome with remorse. It's not modern rock that has grown weak and frail: It is we, the poor old men still trying to camouflage our lack of understanding by claiming there's nothing to be understood. Rock 'n' roll is as healthy as it ever was, the new bands are all just as good as the old ones, and whatever band is on the cover of this week's *Rolling Stone* deserves the honor just as much as the farts who stood there before them.

Yeah. Right.

IN APRIL 2005, the world press was invited to peep inside President George Bush's personal iPod, a birthday gift from his daughters the previous year and, to judge from the wealth of commentary that it provoked, the most intimate glimpse inside the presidential mind that we had ever been given.

Its contents were not really a surprise, even though sundry media commentaries attempted to drum up some kind of controversy around the 250 or so songs stored therein. "No black artists, no gay artists, no world music, only one woman, no genre less than twenty-five years old, and no Beatles," tutted London *Times* reporter Caitlin Moran, as though Bush were the only person in the world not to develop his musical tastes according to the political and sexual orientation of the artist.

A few people did express some shock that the man even had an iPod, let alone the manual dexterity to operate it; comedian Dana Carvey's decade-old impression of Bush as a man more likely to be intrigued by a ball of yarn than by affairs of state continues to color many people's perception of the president. But the music was precisely what you would expect, a sampling of what *Rolling Stone* writer Joe Levy described as "a lot of great artists from the '60s and '70s and more modern artists who sound like great artists from the '60s and '70s," a deduction that was as ultimately unedifying as the musical selection itself.

"Basically," Levy continued, "boomer rock 'n' roll and more recent music out of Nashville made for boomers. It's safe, it's reliable, it's loving. What I mean to say is, it's feel-good music. The Sex Pistols it's not."

I should jolly well hope not.

Any number of modern-day leaders—the most wretched being Britain's former prime minister, the destestable Tony Blair—have gone so far out of their way to court the youth vote and inspire an aura of "hipness" around their sanctified selves that it is a wonder they could even govern any longer, for all the break-dancing that they must surely be doing. But is that a quality that we really want to see in our premiers?

In 1994, the White House opened its doors to its most youthful (as opposed to youngest—nobody would ever describe Teddy Roosevelt as youthful, and JFK was too busy getting laid to worry) incumbent ever, a sax-playing, dope-not-smoking, Cambridge University—attending gentleman named Bill Clinton.

George Bush's iPod: Nine Downloads That Were Certainly Worth the Presidential Ninety-Nine Cents

John Fogerty—"Centerfield"

Van Morrison—"Brown-Eyed Girl"

Stevie Ray Vaughan—"The House Is Rockin'"

The Knack—"My Sharona"

Blackie and the Rodeo Kings—"Swinging From the Chains of Love"

John Hiatt—"Circle Back"

Joni Mitchell—"(You're So Square) Baby, I Don't Care"

Alejandro Escovedo—"Castanets"

Kenny Loggins—"Alive 'N' Kickin'"

The similarly youthful, similarly abstinent, and similarly musical Blair followed three years later, riding a wave of support built upon "Britpop," a musical revival (in every sense of the word) that foisted the likes of Oasis, Blur, and London Suede upon us. Indeed, Blair's rocking credentials were confirmed when it was revealed that he spent at least a portion of his youth playing guitar in a band with a former editor of Q magazine, itself nominally the hippest of all the country's music monthlies.

Further developments, including both men's adoption of sundry rock and pop classics as campaign themes and whatnot, or the steady stream of hip young gunslingers invited into the official residences, there to discuss policy and pop, should not unduly concern us. In a modern world where even the most egregious of errors can be negated if you put enough "spin" on the subject, a couple of pop groups sipping tea with a politician is scarcely the end of the world.

Besides, politicians of every vintage and persuasion have courted the era's most popular entertainers, in the hope that some of the luster will rub off on them. Richard Nixon even asked Elvis to advise him on how to handle America's drug problem; which, given the King's legendary appetites, was a little like asking Jack the Ripper to advise on the placement of a new battered women's shelter.

No, what was at issue here was the fact that, for the first time, our countries were being governed by men who had essentially the same cultural reference points as a large part of their constituency, the baby boomers who were raised on rock, and who still believed that they knew a good pop song when they heard one.

But had the voice of youth finally found a friend in high places? Or had those high places finally figured out how to gag its most vociferous cultural critic? Certainly neither Blair nor Clinton did anything politically to endear themselves to the younger voter, and that despite the creation of a multitude of focus groups establishing that both men "understood" the concerns of the youth. Indeed, Clinton was responsible for signing into law the first of the legislative powers that now encourage record companies to sue their customers for not buying enough new music; and, while Blair seemed poised at one point to decriminalize marijuana, he didn't mean it.

The shadow of a Rod Stewart wig—wearing Uncle Tom loomed large, and the fact that Clinton's successor, George W. Bush, was just forty-four days his senior only exacerbated the uneasiness engendered around the notion that just because somebody *is* young, they must automatically *think* young.

Clinton, for all his personal and political faults, looked, spoke, and sometimes even behaved like somebody who had come of age during the 1960s. Bush, on the other hand, could have been spawned at any time in the previous fifty years. This point was ruthlessly vindicated when the president was spotted (by the *Washington Post*) waving excitedly at Stevie Wonder during a presidential gala at Ford's Theater. Yes, *that* Stevie Wonder. The blind one.

Ten Songs with Rock 'n' Roll in the Title That Don't Suck

Led Zeppelin—"Rock and Roll"

Gary Glitter—"Rock and Roll"

Lou Reed—"Rock 'n' roll"

The Kinks—"A Rock 'n' roll Fantasy"

David Bowie—"Rock 'n' roll Suicide"

Kiss—"Rock 'n' roll All Night"

Grand Funk Railroad—"Rock 'n' roll Soul"

The Arrows—"I Love Rock 'n' roll"

AC/DC—"Rock 'n' roll Damnation"

Jethro Tull—"Too Old to Rock 'n' roll: Too Young to Die!"

and the Other Ten Thousand That Do

Continued on page 224

It is been almost forty years since Pete Townshend first invited us to "meet the new boss, same as the old boss." Back then, he made us swear that we wouldn't get fooled again.

Sorry, Pete.

An artist's best work tends to fall in the earlier years of his career, at that time when he is still hungry, still anxious to prove himself.

Even allowing for the "difficult second album" syndrome, when a band spends so long promoting their debut that they have no time to write songs for the follow-up, the fact is, the music that an artist composes when he's first starting out is automatically destined to resonate far deeper than that penned once his career has started moving, and with infinitely more passion and power than that created when life revolves around nothing more stimulating than the lobby and pool of a hundred identikit hotels. It's one of the reasons why so many bands write songs about their jobs, or unleash incoherent rant after incoherent rant about how rock 'n' roll will save your soul 'cos all the kids wanna boogie.

Good evening, Chattanooga!

There are exceptions to this. Even allowing for the sheer redundancy of trying to convince a field full of sheep that *Sgt. Pepper* really isn't an indisputable masterpiece, few would argue that the first Beatles albums were superior to their "middle" period. Ditto Dylan, the Beach Boys, and the Rolling Stones. But that is because those artists were setting the benchmark by which all others would be measured.

Once that was accomplished, the acts that followed had little choice but to set their own standards by the masters, and work from there. The results, spreading out from around 1966 (debuts by the Velvet Underground and the Mothers of Invention) to 1976 (the farewells to arms discussed elsewhere in this tome) incorporate some of the most spectacular music ever made.

The nature of the modern music industry defies this ruling. Through the 1960s and 1970s, even into the early 1980s, bands did indeed spend their formative years in the figurative garage, testing and retesting their abilities, breaking cover to play the occasional live show in a bar full of people who couldn't care less, then taking the lessons back to headquarters to be assimilated into the act. The concept of a band "paying its dues" has certainly been over-deified in the past, a consequence of the punk movement's obsession with squawking raw immediacy, but still, experience should count for something.

The cycle is broken today. Bands still form as they always did, and still play their first concerts to the ubiquitous audience of three men and a dog, except health and safety regulations tend to leave the dog tied up outside these days, while the smoking ban means that most of the crowd will miss at least part of the show when they pop out for a puff. But the ease with which what was once the most complicated and mystifying recording technology can now be inserted into the home— you don't even need a studio any longer, just a few bucks' worth of software and a decent Internet connection—has seen the gap between first gig and first album reduced to the time it takes to reload the bong.

Which is great from the artist's point of view; it means he or she is ready to roll the moment they've fixed that last dodgy chord progression. It isn't true that the White Stripes' entire first three albums were recorded in the kitchen while Meg was listening to old Robert Plant solo albums on the boom box, but British songbird Lily Allen did launch her mid-2000s career by recording the bulk of her first album at home and then posting the songs to her MySpace page, while compatriot singer-songwriter Sandi Thom rose to local fame on claims (later disproved) that she webcast concerts from her south London flat because she was too poor to actually tour. Stardom without even having to leave your bedroom? There's only one other profession that can offer that.

Now, with no more grinding around the circuit playing the life out of a set of songs, they can be hammered down as soon as they're written, and the artist can move on to the next batch.

But it is positively crippling from an artistic point of view, as songs that should have been given room in which to grow, develop, and turn into something truly special are cemented into recorded immortality the moment they're finished, and the artist has no choice now but to stick with that arrangement for the rest of the number's useful life, because what's the point of still working on a track once it's been thrust into the public view?

It's not as if artists are unaware of this trap. More and more frequently over the past couple of decades, artists have looked back over their earliest releases and admitted outright that "our first album may have been recorded a little too quickly," and that's "quickly" as in too soon after the songs were written, as opposed to following too little time in the studio. Debuts by Led Zeppelin, Black Sabbath, Uriah Heep, and many more were all recorded in a matter of days; days that a modern group would probably have spent trying to get the computerized drum sound right. Or pick up a signal on their mobile phones.

"Can you hear me now?"

It's not a circuit that they are willing, or even permitted, to break. Tell an interested label that you're not ready to record yet and they'll tell you that you probably never will be and then move onto the next week's flavor. So you go along with their demands and turn in something that you know is substandard compared to what it could be, and then they turn around and drop you because it isn't what they wanted.

That dire situation is changing now, as the Internet begins to extend its tentacles into another area that was once the province of the fabulously wealthy and well connected: the manufacture and distribution of the music itself. Even the most savagely independent labels were, until recently, at some point forced to climb into bed with big business, if only to ensure that their product got into stores.

But with the number of stores, too, declining at a terrifying rate, it is apparent that that relationships no longer count for anything. A decade ago, it was considered miraculous that you could even record your new album in your bedroom and have it sound as good as a fully equipped studio could render it. Today you can sell it from there as well, a concept that was first embraced by, among others, Richard Thompson in the late 1990s, but has since been pushed into headline-making functionality by Radiohead.

Is that all we have to look forward to, though? The continued refining of the means by which we *buy* our music, without any regard for what that music actually sounds like?

In 2008, the Dave Matthews Band offered a free live CD to anybody who purchased one of the concert tickets through the Ticketmaster agency. Prince distributed initial copies of his last album via a give-away attached to one of the British Sunday newspapers, and King Kink Ray Davies followed through with much the same notion. (Store-bought copies packed an extra track, but that's not much for the cost of a full CD.)

All of these models are worthy; all help negate the absolute hegemony with which an increasingly tiny cartel of multinational corporations have viewed their fiefdom for far too long. But not one of them addresses the real matter at hand. The fact is, new music sucks, and the means of distribution, ultimately, is irrelevant. It doesn't matter *how* an album winds up in your hands—what counts is whether you'd want it there in the first place.

How many Sonic Youth albums can you play all the way through before you realize that they've now been making the same damned noise for almost thirty years, and that the only thing that separates one disc from the other is how purposefully badly they've recorded it?

Or U2? Once, bands made records that you were proud to love. The kindest thing you could say about U2 at their best is that you have a soft spot for them, and even that dries up once you stop concentrating on the blare of the band, and listen to what Bono's actually saying.

We are invited to care for so many bands today, without any comprehension of whether or not they were worth caring about to begin with. Scott Weiland records a solo album. Great. Any man whose career has taken him from the derivative heights of the Stone Temple Pilots to the derisory mumblings of Velvet Revolver obviously has a lot more to say for himself. My Chemical Romance have cut a concept album. Whoopee!

The Hives have reinvented themselves on their latest platter. Or they have swapped one annoying buzzing sound for another. But don't stop with the Hives. Oasis. Tortoise. Built to Spill. Vampire Weekend. Some of these names have been knocking around your subconscious since the 1990s; most of them will be forgotten by the time you read these words.

It is lazy and, besides, untrue to say that new music does not have new ideas; that it has all been done before. But face it: Radiohead are essentially treading water in a pool of warmed-up King Crimson records, with a touch of Pink Floyd thrown in for variety, and Sigur Rós may be the biggest thing to emerge from Iceland since Bjork first set her fax machine to music, but that does not negate the fact that Tangerine Dream have a lot to answer for.

REM started life and, indeed, spent much of their career, pursuing the gospel according to the Byrds, shot through with just enough questioning grimness to convince impressionable twenty- and thirtysomethings that the band was restating the values of a distant past. Classic rock for a new generation, right? Wrong. The correct word is *recycling*.

Why listen to Of Montreal when you could be playing the Mamas & the Papas? Why bother with Portishead when you still have all those John Barry sound tracks to listen to?

Why even glance toward the modern mess of noughties punk bands when you could track back to the '70s crew and then consign most of them to the dumper as well, because they're just reiterating the same noise that the infant Who, Kinks, and Yardbirds were making?

Devendra Banhart burst onto the scene amid a flourish of ecstatic reviews comparing him to Donovan, Marc Bolan, and the Incredible String Band. Stop there, because why would you need to proceed? Just dig out your old copies of *Sunshine Superman*, *A Beard of Stars*, and *The Hangman's Beautiful Daughter*, and you've just saved yourself the price of hearing them all again.

Have we really become so ecologically conscious that even creativity needs to be recycled all the time? Apparently so.

Yes, you might well feel a thrill of righteous zeal whenever you buy a CD and read that its entire packaging was manufactured from reconstituted copies of last week's newspaper. But so what? Thirty years ago, record companies were recycling unsold vinyl in order to press new releases, and people bitched their backsides off about that!

It's nothing new, and it's nothing to get excited about, because you can bet your ass that they wouldn't be doing it if it affected the bottom line. Their motives might be different today, as might the intentions that they use to justify the process to the shareholders. But that's just this year. Next year, they'll probably have another reason entirely.

Still, there's a world of difference between recycling a CD sleeve to make a brand-new one, and recycling its contents for the same ends, yet the process is now so entrenched that the first thing we ask when someone tells us about a new band is "Great! Who do they sound like?" And we think it's because we need a reference point upon which to hinge our interest, but how facile is that? Mastodon sound like Budgie; I like Budgie; therefore I will like Mastodon.

NO!

How much more exciting would it be to be told, "They sound like nothing on Earth, and if you can think of one past record that they resemble, I'll buy you a box of chocolates." When *Rolling Stone* published its "best of 2007" poll at the end of April 2008, what was your first thought upon seeing Bruce Springsteen and the E Street Band elected "best live act of the year"? Weary resignation? Sad acceptance? Or glorious vindication because it proved that other people are finally seeing through the hollow sham of modern showmanship? Springsteen may or may not be putting on the greatest live show in the world right now. But who would you say is doing it better? Kanye West?

Regularly during the 1970s, and sporadically into the 1980s, new acts would emerge whom one adventurous hack or another would proclaim "the future of rock 'n' roll." It was a lofty title. Springsteen was the first to be saddled with the epithet and, to some extent, he merited it. *Born to Run*, the album to which that comment was initially attached, was indeed a spectacular record, and Springsteen fans will happily point you in the direction of other platters that merit similar platitudes.

But just because it worked once, there was no reason to assume that it would work a second time. Or even a 252nd time. In fact, it is rather fun flicking through back issues of *Creem*, *Melody Maker*, *Trouser Press*, or *Rolling Stone*, seeking out the artists who were being earmarked for glory, and then writing letters to the editor, demanding to know why the entire universe was not now dancing to the sounds of whoever. Moby Grape. Silverhead. Mahogany Rush. Living Colour. Lenny Kravitz. You rarely get a response.

Somewhere around the middle of the 1980s, writers began taking a different tack. Bands were no longer *the* future of rock. They were *an alternate vision of the future of rock*; meaning, it didn't matter whether or not they actually made it out of the garage. For the select handful who bunkered down with their copy of a group's latest record, appreciating it conferred automatic membership in the most exclusive club in the world. And that was yours forever. Eno once said that only a hundred people ever saw the Velvet Underground, and they all went out and formed bands afterward. Imagine if somebody said the same thing about *your* group.

So the shift began. Critics ceased promoting favorite bands for their commercial worth, in favor of lionizing them for their cultural importance. Musicians stopped chasing the poisoned chalice of fame and declared that they enjoyed being poor because the hunger kept them hungry. Or some such nonsense. And, for a while, it worked.

They might not have floated *your* musical boat, but such '80s darlings as Sonic Youth, the Jesus and Mary Chain, and Jane's Addiction were never launched in the belief that they might eventually find fame and fortune, and the fact that they did is neither here nor there. A lot more groups heading out with similar intentions remain as unheard today as they were back then, and even if somebody should reissue their entire back catalog on CD tomorrow, it still won't sell to more than 140 people—all of whom already own the album.

During my own days at *Melody Maker*, during those same dark, drab mid-1980s, I found myself so excited by the debut album by the Len Bright Combo, the snappily titled *The Len Bright Combo Presents the Len Bright Combo by the Len Bright Combo* (I am not making this up), that I genuinely believed (and, in some ways, still do) that if only the entire music industry were held down and forced to actually listen to it, the world would be a very much happier place.

It was a collection of shimmering pop songs, as befit a band fronted by Wreckless Eric, author of the indelibly wonderful "Whole Wide World." But it was recorded so deliberately crudely that "two intensive listens are essential before the dense wall of noise even threatens to make sense. When [they] open 'Young, Upwardly Mobile, and Stupid' a capella, the moment the band comes in sounds like a lift full of fat people falling down a shaft.

"[It] is not an album which sits easily on the turntable. Too many people will take it at face value and dismiss it as the lo-fi ramblings of a demented old rocker. But once you've unlocked the secret of the sound, the Combo's psychotic beat box stands revealed as an album of breathtaking purity, great pop music balanced so far out on the edge that it makes a mockery of the enfants terribles peopling the shock horror pages of today. There isn't another soul in the world with guts enough to release an album as honest as this one. The real world starts here."

They don't make records like that anymore. They didn't really make them like that at the time, either. Remember the first time you listened to *Dark Side of the Moon* on headphones, and jumped when the alarm clocks started chiming through your head? The closest the Len Bright Combo came to stereo was when a barely in-tune organ wandered from speaker to speaker in "Lureland." And when the album was reissued on CD in 2003, it was on Wreckless Eric's own label.

For all of those reasons, I would not expect the majority of the people reading this book to have heard this record. Hell, most of you haven't even heard *of* it. That, however, is not the point. Where *The Len Bright Combo Presents the Len Bright Combo by the Len Bright Combo* stands alone is in the fact that, at the time of its release, and for more than twenty years since then, it was capable of making me feel as though music *mattered* again, with an emotional and physical surge that had been growing all too infrequent as the 1980s progressed, and would become even rarer as further years passed.

You probably have a Len Bright Combo of your own, a guilty pleasure, a special treasure, an album that hits you so hard out of left field, and falls so far from your own musical comfort zone, that you have to keep playing it, just to be sure that it's actually as great as you think.

Something by the Fall, for example. "How are people going to explain Mark E. Smith in fifty years' time?" Elvis Costello once asked, and he's another one, a figure that has never sat still long enough to be nailed to any particular musical cross, and has remained an oasis of redemption because of that. There are probably half a dozen Costello albums (to match the half dozen Fall sets) that kept *somebody* sane through the long, dark night of the past three decades, but it would be futile to try and list all the other artists that have arisen over time to remind you of a day when *all* records were capable of making you feel so good.

Maybe it's an age thing. Nobody born in the pre-Beatles age, who came to musical awareness in the early 1970s, and maturity before the decade's end, could truly feel the same kick inside once they hit their twenties, thirties, forties. It's been said so often that it is virtually a cliché today, but if you haven't discovered the music you love by the time you leave school, the chances are that you never will.

You liked the Cult because they remind you of old Atomic Rooster. You enjoyed Garbage because they kept on making the records that Roxy Music forgot. Counting Crows are terrific if you've never heard Free, and the Polyphonic Spree are absolutely amazing, so long as you remember they aren't the Zombies in disguise. And so on.

But why do you see so many young kids wearing Led Zeppelin T-shirts today? Why is it that the last time the Yardbirds rhythm section toured America, the people who knew the most words to their songs all looked to be under thirty? Explain how the local theater still packs out its weekly midnight showings of *The Rocky Horror Show*? By rights, and by all that's holy, the average age of the audience for all three should be somewhere between forty-five and fifty-five. Instead, it's less than half of that.

Click onto Amazon.com's best-selling albums list for the first week of April 2008: Van Morrison, Jackson Browne, Robert Plant, and the Rolling Stones' Scorsese sound track (and you can bet that it wasn't the opportunity to hear Jagger sing "Live With Me" with Christina Aguilera that brought the orders rolling in), with the now-almost-as-decrepit REM, Madonna, and the B52s close behind.

Across the board, people are rejecting the new music being foisted upon them by the record companies in the pretense that it is somehow relevant and exciting, and making their own choices, from a musical landscape that has never been so vast.

Regardless of whether you approve of them or not, reunions ensure that there is scarcely a key band from the past who cannot be caught at least one more time, while the on-going mania for reissues, remasters, and box sets insists that there's an entire catalog of shiny new CDs sitting out there as well. And if you still can't find what you're looking for, then Google it. Some blog somewhere will have it on file.

In the UK, the readership of *Classic Rock* magazine, with its monthly remit of hard rock and old rockers, has overtaken that of the all-with-it, all-contemporary *New Musical Express*; in the United States, the record-collecting bible *Goldmine* scarcely even acknowledges any artist under the age of sixty, because Pink Floyd will *always* make more hearts race than Panic at the Disco.

Statistics, however, tell only a part of the story, and sales figures can always be twisted to tell whichever story you choose. What really matters is that, across the spectrum, the very value of modern music has been declining in importance for more than thirty years and, no matter how many new acts emerge to try and take up the batons that time has left lying beside the highway, that is all they can ever do—take *up* the baton. They have not created a new one; they have never taken it further.

We are locked, then, in a pattern of absolute disintegration, an ever-narrowing death spiral within which every successive year produces less and less of lasting value, at the same time as the natural attrition of death and decay snatch away more and more of what we truly cherish.

Who, in the middle of the twenty-first century, will the obituary writers describe as his generation's Peter Frampton? Where are the Foghats and Blue Öyster Cults of the 2000s? And what song could possibly come on the radio in the year 2049 and recapture the sights and sounds of today as accurately as "Born to Be Wild" still sums up the world of forty years ago?

Answer those questions and you could cure the malaise that three generations of music fans have lived through, and which each one has declared to be terminal. But ignore them and, sooner or later, somebody's going to notice the smell.

The body's been lying there for a long time, and the stench of corruption clings to it like big-breasted babes around a hair-metal rocker. But even John Doe gets a headstone in the end.

ROCK 'N' ROLL
BORN, MEMPHIS, TN, 1955
DIED, NEGLECT, 1976

BUT NOBODY NOTICED FOR FAR TOO LONG.

Lennon: The Final Comeback

"HECK, HOW WAS I TO KNOW they were falsies? Looked damned real enough to me." John hurled another balled-up piece of paper at a picture of Rick Rubin and looked round the room for support.

He didn't find it. Eyes averted, faces downcast. Even his closest friends—and after this many abortive comebacks, the only people around him were his closest friends—knew that this time, John had blown it. Big-time.

The idea was simple: Three years after his last new record, eight years after his last live performance, and forty years on from his widely exaggerated death, John's career was to be relaunched on the eve of his eightieth birthday with a special guest appearance on the *Ellen DeGeneres Show*. He'd answer a few questions, he'd sing a few songs, and he'd flirt with a few pretty models. Except John being John, he couldn't quit at simply flirting.

"I mean, they just popped! Ruined my outfit. Dammit, wack, I coulda got a shock off my microphone, there was so much water squirting around there. And they ban me from ever appearing on the network again? Fuck, I've got a good mind to buy the network out from under them."

Again, an embarrassed silence. Twenty years ago, he could have. But when the hits stopped, the spending didn't, and "Yoko" didn't help things in the slightest: Anything that John wanted, he'd turn around to "Yoko"—

As I see it, yes.

It is decidedly so.

You may rely on it.

Yes definitely.

Sometimes, his staff were convinced that John had simply rigged the Magic 8-Ball, the one he pasted a picture of his dead wife on, to indulge his every whim.

It had been "Yoko"'s decision to have John hook up with Trent Reznor to record an album of grinding metal standards, *Sometime in New York Hell*, to prove he was still in touch with the kids; "Yoko" told him to wear a sharp studded red leather body suit, the one that shredded the seats in the hired limousine as readily as it punctured that poor girl's pride. Now "Yoko" was sitting smugly on the coffee table, patiently awaiting John's next request. Maybe Julian was right. Maybe they should have the thing exorcised.

Rising unsteadily to his feet, John walked over and switched off the television. In the past, he'd simply have drowned it out with a volley of darkly amusing scouse wit, but that was how low he'd sunk. He'd sold his last joke to pay for studio time and, though the new album had scored a few kindly reviews, if it didn't sell at least a few thousand copies, he might never afford another one.

VH-1 had already turned down the video; apparently graying goatee beards were "last year's thing"; and the best MTV could offer was a round on the recently revitalized *Celebrity Death Match*, Fiona Apple versus the Walrus. John turned them down. "I don't fight women," he told them. "Even scary ones."

"Yoko" had backed him: *Signs point to no.*

"Okay, this is what we'll do. Book Disneyland. Tell 'em I'm done with the death metal stuff, tell 'em I'll just come out whatever they want. Collarless suit, mop-top wig, granny glasses, white piano, whatever, and I'll run through all the hits. Get all the world press there, TV, everyone, then I'll come out in my Richard Nixon costume, rip up the Bill of Rights, duet with Sinead O'Connor, the works. Show the world that you might be able to knock Johnny Lennon down, but you can never make him stay there."

Julian sighed as loudly as the latest plastic surgery job would allow him to. He might not have inherited Sean's looks or business sense, but he was the only person left whom John even listened to these days. "Or you could apologize to Paul."

"Never," interrupted John.

"Apologize to your Paul for all those horrible things you said about *Ram*, and let him write and produce another record for you. That's all he's waiting for, you know. And don't say you'd rather be homeless than say sorry, because the way things are going, you probably will be."

John's eyes flashed. For a moment, Julian saw the cocky, arrogant, street-smart scrapper who had won his mom's heart all those years ago back in the pool. But only for a moment. Then the angry old man returned, with that crooked, devious smile Julian had long since grown to despise. "You may be right. We'll let 'Yoko' decide."

But Julian knew what she would answer before John even posed the question, so he didn't even try. Instead, he tossed her out of the window and glared defiantly back at his father. "She said she needed some air."

The room was silent, all eyes fixed on John. He, too, seemed lost in thought, and the only question was, What was he thinking? Then, as he turned and left the room, Where was he going? "Yoko," they knew, would have been dashed to a million pieces, leaking thick blue fluid across the sidewalk eight floors down, her multifaceted mind just a lump of useless plastic. Julian was just stepping toward the window to make certain, when John returned to the room.

"You're right. She was old. She was only ever out for herself. The only person a man can really trust is his mother." In his hand he held

183

a plastic doll, her factory face replaced with a faded, smiling photograph. When you turned her upside down, she spoke.

"Yes, dear. Of course, dear. Whatever you think is best, dear." John, too, smiled. "Julian? Julia wants you to call Walt Disney."

The Classic Rock Manifesto: She Gets the Blokes Because She Smokes

1.♦ WE DECLARE UNEQUIVOCALLY that the phrase is "rock 'n' roll." It is not "rock AND roll," nor "rock & roll," nor any other variation. Ignorance of this law will not be tolerated, although dispensation is permitted to the retrospective transgressions committed by Led Zeppelin, Gary Glitter, and Kiss.

2.♦ WE INJUNCT ALL ROCK 'N' ROLL BANDS to employ a basic lineup of vocals, guitar, bass, and drums. Keyboards are acceptable, as are flutes and electric violins, provided they are neither overbearing nor employed as a substitute for one of the above (the Doors and ELP notwithstanding). Cellos and other orchestral pieces must be employed cautiously, as must those instruments borrowed from other cultural disciplines. One sitar-led song per album maximum.

3.♦ WE CELEBRATE every valid opportunity for the kids to be encouraged to boogie (except on those occasions when they should rock, rock 'n' roll, or rock out). But there shall be no gratuitous overuse of these terms; nor of the phrases "a wop bop a loo bop," "be bop a lula," or similar lyrical devices. If a song is worth singing, it shall first of all make sense (cf: Bob Dylan, John Lennon, Bryan Ferry) unless it does not need to (cf: "Stairway to Heaven").

4. WE RECOMMEND that self-pity be avoided wherever possible, unless a definite purpose is met by the exposition. (cf: Leonard Cohen, *Blood on the Tracks*, and sundry acceptable sad songs).

5. WE PROHIBIT all mention of the term "rehab," or any vernacular variation, insinuation, or suggestion. Public discussion of the "benefits" extended by these facilities is likewise prohibited, as is the use, actual or intended, of "rehab" facilities.

6. WE FIRMLY and unwaveringly believe that drugs are there to be taken, according to the dreams and desires of the taker. Likewise alcohol, cigarettes, and the willingly distributed favors of sexual partners.

7. HOWEVER, WE WOULD PREFER it if you didn't keep writing songs about it.

8. WE DEMAND that all guitars are fed through amplifiers only. A selection of pedals is permissible for emphasis, effect, and Joe Walsh impersonations. Synthesizers, keyboards, and similar electronic devices are prohibited.

9. WHERE SYNTHESIZERS ARE PERMITTED, it is for the construction of sounds including, but not necessarily restricted to, whooshing, bleeping, and farting noises. Remember at all times that the synthesizer, and all similar electronic gadgets, is a tool, and should not be a replacement for any other instrument.

10. WE RECOMMEND THAT, when speaking with the press, conversation be kept to musical themes, with cultural, political, and similarly controversial themes employed only if the writer is an absolute moron, or you are trying to get up Bono's nose. Or you are Neil Young.

11. THE RIFF IS ALL and all are the riff. Hail the riff and praise and venerate it at all times.

12. BUT AGAIN, don't overdo it.

13. IT IS UNANIMOUSLY believed that clothes should for the most part be loosely fitting garments of denim, sheepskin, or leather, except for trousers purposefully designed to accentuate manliness, which should nevertheless allow for the additional insertion of up to three pairs of groin socks.

14. THOSE JACKETS with the long hanging fringes on the arms are okay as well.

15. IT IS PROSCRIBED that all bands release no fewer than two albums of studio material before recording and releasing a double live album.

16. WHEREVER POSSIBLE and whenever practical, long-term relationships should be confined to partners who appear grounded to the reality of everyday life (cf: Cynthia Lennon, Dee Harrington, Maureen Starkey). The accompaniment of leggy models, glamorous actresses, and sundry other large-busted babes should be confined to gala openings, video shoots, and movie premiers wherever possible (cf: Britt Ekland, Bebe Buell, etc.).

17. WE IMPLORE YOU never to place your musical or personal support behind any politician. Even the truthful ones are ultimately untrustworthy, for why else would they want to enter politics in the first place? Especially beware of those that court you first.

18. FINALLY, WE REQUEST all patrons to leave the premises as noisily and controversially as possible. Remember, this is rock 'n' roll, not the Young Republicans Dinner, Dance, and Mixer. You are meant to be a bad example. So be one. The cherry bombs are in the third drawer on the right; the bathroom is the second door on the left. And the mud sharks are in the tank in the main reception.

The Top 100 Classic Rock Songs, 1968–1976

HE GREAT THING ABOUT LISTS, particularly lists that claim to represent the Top Whatever of Something, is that very few people agree with them. The great thing about *this* list is, nobody cares what you think. I polled my friends, I surfed the 'net, I read magazines, and I listened to the radio, and every single one of them disagreed with something or other. I don't care. The following list has been compiled *not* from the most popular songs in the classic rock catalog (although most of them are), nor from the most played (although many of them are). The songs here are those that best represent what classic rock should be, and what so few songs recorded since this time actually are. So complain away and make your own lists, and if you post them to our website at http://www[webaddresstocome], we will probably delete them without a second thought. Because if there is one thing that this book has taught us, it's not that opinions are like assholes. It's that assholes like opinions. Especially their own. So rock on, my little snowflakes, and if you have room for just a hundred more songs on your MP3 player, make it these. Your soul will thank you.

1. Led Zeppelin—"Stairway to Heaven"

"It was a milestone for us," Robert Plant said in 1975. "Every musician wants to do something of lasting quality, something which will hold up for a long time, and I guess we did it with 'Stairway.'"

A pagan love song that became the most played, and most requested, song in the history of American rock radio; the ultimate youth club slow dance; the best-selling single piece of sheet music in history; the absolute zenith of Led Zeppelin's folk-rock hybrid; and an epic that was *still* as dizzying a kaleidoscope in 2007, when Zeppelin included it in their reunion repertoire, as it was when it first entered their live set, following the release of *Led Zeppelin IV* in 1970.

True, when *Rolling Stone* published its Top 500 songs of all time, "Stairway to Heaven" did not even make the Top 30; and, it is said, if you should ever play it backwards, you will hear Zeppelin praising Satan (the exact words are open to interpretation, but they are generally assumed to go like this: "Oh, here's to my sweet Satan / The one whose little path would make me sad, whose power is Satan / He will give those with him 666 / There was a little toolshed where he made us suffer, sad Satan").

But it made Duran Duran cry when it was played at Zeppelin's 1985 Live Aid reunion, and there isn't any song that could even threaten to knock it off the top of this list.

CLASSIC ROCK MOMENT (CRM): 5:56—Guitar solo comes in.

2. The Who—"Won't Get Fooled Again"

The closing track from the Who's 1971 *Who's Next* album, "Won't Get Fooled Again" is still the fiercest denunciation of party-line politics ever set to music. It's not just the force of the lyric that hits you (although few songs have ever so accurately captured that same sense of exhausted betrayal); the band's performance matches it word for word, as Pete Townshend's best-ever power chords do battle with the fidgety agitation of a synthesized organ, before vocalist Daltrey and drummer Moon resolve the conflict for all time with what has to stand as the most dramatic finale of any song, ever.

CRM: 7:45—And the primal scream to end them all.

3. Eagles—"Hotel California"

Released in 1976, "Hotel California" opened the Eagles' first new album since the recruitment of guitarist Joe Walsh. One of the band's most thoughtful efforts (matched only by the same album's epic closer, "The Last Resort"), it imbibes the titular state with the same dramatic foreboding that you feel when you think about the passengers boarding the *Titanic*.

But it's the epic guitar coda, Walsh and Don Felder in full dueling-banjos mode, that truly transforms "Hotel California," driving it from lament to statement in less time than it takes to cross the parking lot, while giving the listener more time to think about the words. Felder, who cowrote the song with Don Henley, later admitted he was dead set against it being released as a single: "It's six minutes long; it breaks down and stops in the middle; [and] you can't dance to it." It also sounds a lot like Jethro Tull's "We Used to Know," but hey, accidents happen.

CRM: 3:52—Kill the beast!

4. Queen—"Bohemian Rhapsody"

Three weeks in the studio and more than two hundred vocal overdubs were required to bring Freddie Mercury's vision to life, and it would be difficult to think of a more *un*-single-like single to release by a band that was still only just breaking even, critically and commercially. But "Bohemian Rhapsody" went on to top the UK chart for six weeks in 1975, and for another five in the aftermath of Freddie Mercury's death in 1991, while it has been topping sundry "best British single" polls almost since its release. The odd thing is, no matter how easy it is to describe the song as a mini-opera, the segment in question lasts just a minute. The balladic outro is almost as long.

CRM: 3:08—Here come the operatics.

5. Don McLean—"American Pie"

Too long in its original form for a single, "American Pie" was sliced in two for 45 release, but radio delighted in airing the full version regardless. The title song of McLean's second album, "American Pie" tells the tale of America's musical life from the death of Buddy Holly ("the day the music died": February 3, 1959) to the murder of Meredith Hunter at Altamont in December 1969; a tumultuous decade that ends with McLean already mourning the music's loss of innocence. But when he was asked outright what the song meant to him, he replied, "It means I never have to work again."

CRM: 1:30—"Did you write the book of love?"

6. Derek and the Dominos—"Layla"

Packing perhaps the most impassioned vocal of Eric Clapton's entire career, but driven by the twin guitar attack of Clapton and friend Duane Allman, the title track from the one and only album by this exercise in anonymity was a straightforward love song for girlfriend (later wife) Patti Boyd. The title was borrowed from the epic Persian poem "The Story of Layla."

CRM: 0:41—So many to choose from, beginning with the moment the vocal first cracks into view, through to the mood-shifting transition from riff to piano. But the first chorus hits you like a ton of bricks every time.

7. Gary Glitter—"Rock and Roll Part Two"

"Rock and Roll" is the tribal war cry of the twentieth century. Forget its absorption into American sporting iconography; forget, too, the fact that Gary built a five-year career at the top of the British charts just by recycling that same primeval formula. You can even forget that, thanks to sundry personal indiscretions, Glitter is widely considered a leper in his homeland. "Rock and Roll" is important because of its lyrics; and those lyrics, the most joyful, meaningful, and utterly, defiantly, triumphant lyrics in the entire history of modern music, go "Rock 'n' roll, rock 'n' roll, rock 'n' roll, rock 'n' roll." That's part one, anyway. Part two is even better. That one goes, "Hey, hey, hey, hey, hey." Who needs "a-wop-bop-a-loo-bop"? Who cares for "since my baby left me"? Talk about rock 'n' roll, and you only need to say one thing. "Rock 'n' Roll." Hey!

CRM: 2:10—The leader screams amidst the grunts.

8. Black Sabbath—"Iron Man"

The early Black Sabbath was more or less established on the power of the riff, and the *Paranoid* album packs some of the greatest ever coined: The title track and "War Pigs" both vie for supremacy, but it's "Iron Man" that wins out, not only by virtue of the guitar line but also through the inclusion of an equally memorable melody. If *Beavis and Butt-head* didn't rip on this song, they should have.

CRM: 0:28—The riff at the end of the world.

9. Iron Butterfly—"In a Gadda Da Vida"

Jeff Beck was staggered the first time he saw Iron Butterfly, in 1967. "I wouldn't go round handing out gold-plated posters about them on the musical side, but what knocked me out is that the whole of their [set] was devoted to just one number. They spun it out for around thirty-five minutes!" On vinyl, the same song was reined in at around half that length, but listening to it remained a feat of startling endurance, particularly once the drum solo kicked in.

CRM: 12:39—That moment when all the solo gymnastics have finally been put on the shelf, and the signature riff begins building again.

10. Bob Dylan—"Tangled Up in Blue"

Dylan once said he wrote the song after spending a weekend listening to Joni Mitchell's *Blue* album, which might well be true. A triumphant, if occasionally opaque, opening to the otherwise-less-than-exuberant *Blood on the Tracks*, "Tangled Up in Blue" features what is simultaneously one of Dylan's most perfectly realized lyrics, and the one that he seems the least happy with; regular twists and fiddles have seen "new" versions appear on a regular basis, with 1984's *Real Live* album delivering a new set of words altogether. (Although it is quite possible that the song was traveling incognito. That really wasn't a very good record.)

CRM: 0:00—Dylan doesn't really do "classic rock moments," but when a song fits, you know it.

11. Bruce Springsteen—"Born to Run"

It sounds as though he's singing the entire song on one breath of air and, if you don't pay attention to the lyrics, that Tourette's-like helter-skelter of street-racers, girls, and car parts, you can see why Patti Smith once called Springsteen the sexiest mumbler she'd ever heard. The song that launched a thousand legends and a million impersonators, all wrapped up in less time than it took Iron Butterfly's drummer to find a beat.

CRM: 3:05—Counting the band in and exploding.

12. Rolling Stones—"Sympathy for the Devil"

Beggars Banquet is the archetypal Stones album, at least so far as the band's late 1960s/early 1970s public image is concerned. From start to finish, the ten songs fit like a glove: the brutal sexuality of "Stray Cat Blues," the urban violence of "Street Fighting Man," the badlands hoedown of "Prodigal Son"—these songs merged so perfectly with the Stones' public persona that their sentiments became utterly inseparable. But "Sympathy for the Devil" was the terrifying apogee, a lyric that Jagger wrote after reading Soviet author Mikhail Bulgakov's *The Master and Margarita*, but which was far easier to view as unadorned autobiography. Even today, as many legends and myths adhere to "Sympathy for the Devil" as the rest of the band's output put together.

CRM: 2:49—The owls are hooting and the guitar scythes in like napalm.

13. Led Zeppelin—"Trampled Underfoot"

The song is about an automobile . . . or, at least, a woman who does not seem to mind being compared to one. But it hit the dance floors like a bulldozer, frantic guitar and drop-dead rhythm, and it didn't let up, five and a half minutes of such compulsive, copulating frenzy that, even when you think you're going to get some respite, it's only the song taking a breath. It comes back just as wild straight after.

CRM: 0:05—Bonzo's most economical drum solo (three beats and you're in) ignites the most hyperactive version of "Long Train Running" you've ever not recognized.

14. Aerosmith—"Dream On"

They should have recorded it with a full choir, they should have asked Steve Tyler to put a bit more oomph into his vocal, and they should never have allowed the Mission to record the definitive version. But if you have a cigarette lighter handy, you're already waving it.

CRM: 0:54. It's the chorus. Of course it's the chorus.

15. Deep Purple—"Smoke on the Water" (live)

"Smoke on the Water" represented the first occasion upon which Frank Zappa and the Mothers of Invention got their name into the American Top 40. It was they who were onstage when the Montreux Casino burned down (Purple were merely in the audience), the event that inspired the band to take a riff they'd abandoned a few days before and transform it into a legend.

Twenty-five years later, bassist Roger Glover joked, "The new name of the band, by the way, is 'Deep Purple Oh Yes "Smoke on the Water" I Went to College With That.' The funny thing is, when *Machine Head* came out, the song we thought was going to be big was 'Never Before.' We put a lot of work into that, a nice middle eight, polished performances, properly mixed." He's right, too. The studio version frankly is a bit of a drag, but caught on the definitive *Made in Japan* live set, "Smoke" steams.

CRM: 3:55—The return of the riff.

16. Fleetwood Mac—"Rhiannon"

The cause of more arguments than any other record on this list, but who cares? Stevie Nicks' saga of a Welsh witch remains one of the era's most evocative soft rockers, and the only regret is that Mac never got round to releasing the eight-plus-minute version that highlighted period live shows. Lindsey Buckingham gives the guitar all he's got, Nicks is singing in tongues, and the fact that the CRM practically falls at the end of the studio fade-out just shows how phenomenal the concert version was.

CRM: 3:51—Dreams start unwinding and so, on stage, does Nicks.

17. Edgar Winter Group—"Frankenstein"

Funky jazz-rock meets the mad scientist, and look out, kids, he's just built a synthesizer!

CRM: 2:22—The drum solo begets the synth solo begets the freak-out begets chaos.

18. Peter Frampton—"Show Me the Way"

The *Frampton Comes Alive* version, naturally. Has anybody ever even heard the original studio take?

CRM: 0:20—It has to be the thing that he does with his mouth box. The first time, before everybody else joined in.

19. Lynyrd Skynyrd—"Freebird"

Written as a tribute to departed Allmans Duane Allman and Berry Oakley, but spouting wings of its own the moment it got out there, "Freebird" topped so many "best song" polls during the mid-1970s that you actually started to dread ever hearing it again. But then you did, and you could forgive it anything.

CRM: 4:43—The Lord knows he can't change. But he does anyway. The guitars don't leave him any option.

20. Blue Öyster Cult—"Don't Fear the Reaper"

"It's basically a love song where the love transcends the actual physical existence of the partners," vocalist/author Buck Dharma explained, and everybody who thought that BÖC should have more pressing things to write about (secret treaties, tyranny, mutation, and ME 262s for a start) was swept away by the unrelenting tide of support that now gathered around that serpentine riff. In later years, *Saturday Night Live* would reinvent the song as little more than a vehicle for the barely noticeable cowbell that features in the intro, a sketch that the modern BÖC have embraced with creakingly depressing grace.

CRM: 3:23—The arty instrumental break comes to a close and then the guitar riff slices back into view.

21. Steppenwolf—"Born to Be Wild"

Kicking off the self-titled debut album by Canadian-American hard rockers Steppenwolf, en route to a starring role in the era-defining *Easy Rider* movie, "Born to Be Wild" remains one of the most quintessential records of its ilk, and not just for the air of outlaw defiance that ricochets between its pounding chords and riffs. Personally, I've always preferred Slade's live version; far ballsier, far longer, and the singer doesn't sound so much like he's holding down a day job at a carpet warehouse. But that's just me. Whoever it's by, it's always going to get your motor running.

CRM: Seriously? It's the whole thing.

22. Blue Cheer—"Summertime Blues"

Coming on like the most delinquent juveniles ever allowed to stack a pile of Marshalls up in daddy's garage, and heavier than most bands three times their age, Blue Cheer don't so much perform the song as trample on its vital organs and make a lot of noise while they're at it. "Incorrigible" doesn't even begin to describe it.

CRM: 0:37—The first time they forget the last line of the verse.

23. Rolling Stones—"Brown Sugar"

Opening *Sticky Fingers*, the third and final installment in the Stones' triumvirate of defining triumphs (following *Beggars Banquet* and *Let It Bleed*), "Brown Sugar" became the band's first new single since "Honky Tonk Women," almost two years earlier, and ignited their 1970s catalog around one of the most leviathan riffs of the age.

Purists insist that better versions of the song remain in the vault (bootlegs notwithstanding, of course), but still it is hard to resist the twin guitar riffery that kicks the performance into motion, and a lyric that hints at all manner of depravities without taking a single social liberty. Well, not many, anyway.

CRM: 1:39—The riff is the song, and the lyrics leave you bleeding. But that sax break is the key all the same.

24. Greg Allman—"Midnight Rider"

On the road with his very last silver dollar, Gregg sounds desperate enough to do anything. Or maybe he's already done it. A lot of folk have flaunted outlaw chic as a way of life, but Allman was one of the first to make it sound a little less than fun.

CRM: 0:24—That opening, plaintive, drawling wail.

25. ELP—"Lucky Man"

Of all the songs in all the bars in all the world, why did you put this one on the jukebox? The most mystifyingly popular ELP song of them all: There are so many that are better than this. But fifty million radio DJs cannot be wrong. And the lucky man? He was the guy who died before he heard it.

CRM: 3:22—The keyboard whooshing that reminds you this isn't James Taylor.

26. Aerosmith—"Walk This Way"

It's probably impossible to listen to this without immediately replaying the Run DMC revision that relaunched Aerosmith's career in the mid-1980s. But still a swaggering slice of arrogant nastiness supreme.

CRM: 0:32—The first time you think Tyler is going to sing the chorus, and the guitar kicks in instead.

27. Chicago—"25 or 6 to 4"

If Crosby, Stills & Nash were abducted by jazz-rock-loving aliens, and forced to play a free festival in space, this would be the song that saved them from a fate worse than even the Belfegorian Wartsnurkers had in store for them. It's complete twaddle, but it is irresistibly virtuoso twaddle all the same. That guitar solo!

CRM: 3:16—And, when the solo ends, the bass line rattles the floorboards.

28. Boston—"More Than a Feeling"

Do you remember the first time you ever heard "More Than a Feeling"? You woke up one morning, the sun was doing something or other, and you turned on some music to fill your head. Lost yourself in a song. Closed your eyes. Slipped away . . . It started slowly, the lilting tangle of acoustic and electric guitars, a few gentle lines about nothing in particular, just another pleasant ballad, and then the guitars kicked in, a riff screamed into view, and the song soared to the kind of peak that most bands reserve for their final moments. Then it dropped back. Then it returned. Then it went away. Then there was a solo, soaring and howling and, though the lyric seemed to be nothing more than another blast of nostalgia, the memories invoked by an oldie on the radio, you knew there and then what that record was. It was "More Than a Feeling," self-referential, self-reverential, and utterly self-perpetrating.

CRM: 0:42—You know *exactly* which bit it is. And, if you don't, ask Nirvana.

29. Rod Stewart—"Maggie May"

"Wake up, Maggie!" That opening line gets you every time, grabs you by the heart and drags you into a ballad that is half-confessional and half-drunken boasting, the younger man ensnared by a woman twice his age, and seduced so hard that he might not ever get away. It's a love song, to be sure, but not one that you would ever want to be on the receiving end of.

CRM: 0:15—The twiddly little guitar intro sets you up for a lot of things, but the door bursting open and a drummer falling into the room probably isn't one of them.

30. Fleetwood Mac—"Go Your Own Way"

The signature hit of Christmas 1976, prefacing the ubiquitous smash of 1977, the mega-million-selling *Rumours* album, "Go Your Own Way" is usually regarded as a Lindsey Buckingham tour de force. But then you blot out the rest of the song (which is a little annoying, to be truthful) and listen to the drums . . . just the drums . . . only the drums. If this isn't Mick Fleetwood's greatest ever performance, then it's damned close, and he drags the rest of the band along for the ride.

CRM: 2:53—Buckingham's been threatening a solo all song long, but still that shift in tone when it happens catches you by surprise.

31. Led Zeppelin—"Whole Lotta Love"

A great song when the Small Faces invented it, a great riff by the time Zep had finished revising it, but still more of a feeling than a favorite. The experimental passage in the middle is especially galling, schizo-phrenic bumblebees swarming while Plants gets ready to sneeze, but then the drums and guitar hit back and sweep them all away.

CRM: 0:36—The first time the guitar cuts like a razor across the chorus.

32. Lynyrd Skynyrd—"Sweet Home Alabama"

Hook-laden riffs that draw you into a slice of Southern pride that has nothing to do with the negative stereotypes that Neil Young (name-checked within) associated with the lifestyle. "Sweet Home Alabama" wanders disconsolately across the contemporary American landscape, and then comes to the same conclusion that it started out with: There's no place like home.

CRM: 0:06—The voice that tells them to "turn it up." It's what you should do with all great records.

33. Lou Reed—"Sweet Jane" (live)

The *Rock 'n' roll Animal* version isn't quite the best rendition Reed has ever released—that pleasure opens 1978's *Take No Prisoners* live album in a hail of abuse and ad-libs. But if you want one you can dance, sing, or screw to, this is it.

CRM: 3:20—The Steve Hunter—Dick Wagner guitar partnership is soloing so sweetly that you forget whose show this even is. Then Lou swaggers out, the crowd gives a roar, and here comes that riff.

34. Vanilla Fudge—"You Keep Me Hanging On"

Drawing the Supremes classic out to preposterous lengths, then imbuing it with kaleidoscopic moods, the Fudge spread the drama so liberally across the grooves that the song is practically a soap opera. The inescapable blueprint for every prog band of the next two or three years, it proved an albatross for the Fudge (who never scaled such peaks again), but was the self-confessed launching pad for the early Deep Purple.

CRM: 5:56—The ghost of the melody rising from nowhere to haunt a single organ passage.

35. Led Zeppelin—"Rock and Roll"

Electric adrenaline pouring helter-skelter across pell-mell guitars, ADD drums, and Plant's most hyper-adrenalized vocal—a self-affirming celebration of everything that rock 'n' roll could ever mean, what else could they have titled it?

CRM: 0:07—The moment where the drum intro gives way to the full band.

36. Pink Floyd—"Money"

It seems strange to hear "Money" falling out of the sequence that *Dark Side of the Moon* demands, but it's only when it is in isolation that you realize just what a great, and so compulsive, rock song it is.

CRM: 0:26—Past the cash registers, past the bass riff, to the first slash of Dave Gilmour's guitar.

37. Elton John—"Funeral for a Friend/Love Lies Bleeding"

Whooshing synths, stately piano, somber guitar: You can see the mists swirl round the gravestones, the mourners' heads all bent in silence. . . . If music were in color, "Funeral for a Friend" would be grays and blacks. Even when the rest of the band steps in, the mood doesn't lift. "Love Lies Bleeding" shifts the tempo somewhat, but even classic rock 'n' roll sounds dignified after that intro.

CRM: 3:32—The crescendo's been building for an age, and then there's a sudden downstroke, a change of pace, and that guitar steps in with such stately aplomb that it could be accompanying royalty.

38. Focus—"Hocus Pocus"

Focus' own Thijs van Leer notwithstanding, one struggles to think of a single rock artist who was able to carve a career out of the ability to yodel. But one can examine the vocal techniques of a plethora of subsequent front people, from the Talking Heads' David Byrne and XTC's Andy Partridge through Lene Lovich, Kate Bush, and Perry Farrell, and wonder how many hours they spent trying to sing along to "Hocus Pocus"? And that's both the vocal interludes and the instrumental breaks.

CRM: 1:14—The first time the yodeling ends and the band comes in with a vengeance. It's the moment when you realize that rock has just sped off to another planet entirely.

39. Pink Floyd—"Time"

See "Money" (previous page). Except "Time" has an even better guitar solo.

CRM: 2:14—You sit through an intro that perfectly encapsulates the song's world-weary subject matter, but then you hit the moment where the first vocal ignites.

40. Elton John—"Bennie and the Jets"

The mythological saga of a nonexistent band, the ultimate glam combo seen through the eyes of the most unlikely pop star of his generation (come on, then, you name another world-famous, prematurely bald, plump bisexual named Reg?), set to a pseudo-live backdrop that sends the excitement level skyrocketing.

CRM: 3:00—That first glimpse of Elton's falsetto.

41. The Who—"Behind Blue Eyes"

Resolutely unexciting but utterly captivating regardless, Pete Townshend's lament for the misunderstood artiste wrung out one of Roger Daltrey's most passionate vocals.

CRM: 2:19—The hint of an instrumental break that declares a complete change in tempo.

42. Rolling Stones—"You Can't Always Get What You Want"

This sound piece of advice from Mom and Pop Stone seems to have been hijacked for so many other multimedia purposes that it's easy to forget it's a song about trying to score in Swinging London . . . but then you check out the choirboys' pronunciation! *Glarsss* for "glass," *caarnt* for "can't"—it's like *Masterpiece Theatre* for junkies.

CRM: 4:30—That marvelous moment in the instrumental break when the choir chimes in with celestial passion.

43. Rolling Stones—"Gimme Shelter"

Foreboding, forbidding, and chilling, even before you heard the lyrics, "Gimme Shelter" looked around at the state of America in the last years of the '60s and emerged pregnant instead with all the menace that seemed to be gathering round the Stones. Two years after, "Gimme Shelter" would be lifted for the title of the Stones' *Altamont* movie, and that has colored its reputation even further. Even before that, it was uneasy listening.

CRM: 2:43—Merrie Clayton's backing vocals step into the spotlight on their own, and perfection isn't even a kiss away any longer.

44. Johnny Winter—"Rock 'n' Roll Hoochie Koo"

A good ol' boy anthem that makes a lot of noise about nothing in particular, but still manages to kick you in the pituitary gland.

CRM: 1:48—The yell!

45. Allman Brothers—"Jessica"

One of those charming instrumental shuffles that every Southern guitar band seemed to have, but there was something hauntingly resonant about "Jessica" that none of the others ever touched.

CRM: 1:39—A bridge of sighing gentility breaking the song in half, before it picks up in exactly the same place it left off.

46. Pink Floyd—"Wish You Were Here"

From the 1975 LP of the same name, another downbeat rumination on the meaning of life, and this one doesn't get any cheerier, no matter how long it goes on. But hey, we can't be happy all the time, can we?

CRM: 2:04—That moment when the band crashes in around the lone Waters vocal.

47. Doobie Brothers—"Black Water"

Two songs in one, the first a slightly swampy romp through the catfish-infested Mississippi, with a gentle hook that just oozes gumbo and fiddles; the second, the seemingly random selection of a lyric that you barely noticed the first time around, elevated into one of the most compulsive chants of the age.

CRM: 3:09—The moment when the barbershop harmonies kick in.

48. ELP—"Karn Evil Nine First Impression Part Two"

The title gives away the sheer protracted madness of this, the key cut on ELP's *Brain Salad Surgery* album, but the slice-and-dice approach to the movements betrays one of the most cohesive epics of the age, travelling from a sci-fi carnival where the universe is your oyster to the last words that a technocratic future will ever allow you to hear. The *Terminator* movies could have started here. The world that they illustrate still might.

CRM: 0:05—Welcome back, my friends! On vinyl, the natural break as you turned over the disc (part one closed side one) completely set you up for that opening line. CD blunts the experience somewhat, but the fission is still there

49. Santana—"Black Magic Woman"

A minor hit for composer Peter Green's Fleetwood Mac, "Black Magic Woman" is nevertheless synonymous with Santana, whose 1970 cover took them to number four, the band's biggest ever single. "Did you know," Green once asked, "Santana received an award for over two million plays all over the States for their version of that? And Fleetwood Mac's might get a spin once or twice for kicks."

CRM: 1:07—Skip across the intro and it's that moment where the vocal just falls into place.

50. Golden Earring—"Radar Love"

One of the greatest motorvatin' songs of all time, "Radar Love" is up there with Chuck Berry and "Roadrunner" in the Automotive Hall of Rock 'n' roll Fame. Vocalist Barry Hay wrote the lyric while brainstorming with a friend who was vacationing from the US. "It had to be something very simple, to which every average person could relate. The idea of an ordinary guy in his car began to take shape." The friend left to visit a local nightclub; by the time he returned, the song was finished. The friend went wild, Hay remembered. "Brilliant! The ultimate American car song!" Of course, he was correct.

CRM: 1:19—How do you choose? Like highway milestones, every moment means something to someone. But that first "we got a thang" will do it every time.

51. Bachman Turner Overdrive— "You Ain't Seen Nothing Yet"

The Who had already delivered the last w-w-w-word in stuttering, but the Canadian BTO updated it for the hard rock age and coupled it with that riff was a stroke of absolute genius.

CRM: 0:45—She looked at me with big brown eyes and said you ain't *heard* nothing yet either.

52. Guess Who—"American Woman"

As protest songs go, this one really did seem somewhat obtuse, and the lilting acoustic intro completely throws you for a loop. But then the riff comes in, and the antiwar dance starts here.

CRM: 1:30—UGH!

53. Led Zeppelin—"Kashmir"

Following "Trampled Underfoot" off the *Physical Graffiti* album, "Kashmir" is Robert Plant's choice for the "definitive" Led Zeppelin number, and it's certainly one of their most ambitious. Phased percussion and Page's unlikely tuning (DAGDAD) combine with a mood that Plant slipped into while driving from Goulimine to Tantan, in Morocco. "The whole inspiration came from the fact that the road went on and on and on. It was a single-track road, which neatly cut through the desert. Two miles to the east and west were ridges of sand rock. It basically looked like you were driving down a channel, this dilapidated road, and there was seemingly no end to it."

CRM: 0:54—The sound of the band getting into gear, readying themselves for the long haul.

54. Bruce Springsteen—"Jungleland"

The greatest of all Brooooooce's street-suite epics, the ultimate American dream—turned-nightmare resets *West Side Story* on the New Jersey Turnpike, where pianos tinkle to the clash of switchblades and every lyric chases the hungry and the hunted round the parking lot battlefield. And don't miss the ghost of "Sweet Jane" flirting around the instrumental break.

CRM: 8:00—You have to sit through a lot before it finally arrives, but there's a density to the upcoming verse that might be the most honest Springsteen has ever sounded.

55. Crosby, Stills, Nash & Young—"Ohio"

Neil Young's uneasy partnership with Crosby, Stills, and Nash was at its peak when four Kent State students were shot and killed by National Guardsmen policing an antiwar demonstration on the college campus, and there are few more stirring moments in their (or any other contemporary) catalog than this. Even more impressively, the outrage still rings loudly today, whether pealing from the original 45 or, even more impressively, folding from Young's *Journey Through the Past* sound track, as Stephen Stills' equally stirring "Find the Cost of Freedom" slips poignantly into Young's lament.

CRM: 0:26—"Tin soldiers and Nixon coming." Has there ever been a more powerful opening line? Not in 1970 there hadn't.

56. Brownsville Station—"Smoking in the Boys Room"

Cub Koda & Co. kick out with one of the all-time crucial school's *in* anthems, immature glitter rock stamping its feet to a hard metal beat.

CRM: 0:00—The title, the sentiment, the lot. You don't even need to play the record to know why this one matters.

57. Doobie Brothers—"Long Train Running"

You forget what a funky little monster this is, just how close it came to the dreaded disco, two years before anybody even knew to be scared of such a thing. Over the next couple of years, Robert Palmer, Hall & Oates, David Bowie, and Roxy Music would all rise up to take the credit for knocking rock onto the dance floor, but the Doobies really did do it first.

CRM: 0:17—The first slash of vocal.

58. Steely Dan—"Do It Again"

If they weren't the most soporific superstars of the age, then we must have slept through everybody else. But "Do It Again" is as compulsive as school and as memorable as Christmas, and all it really needs is a tune.

CRM: 1:38—The chorus.

59. Jethro Tull—"Locomotive Breath"

So many nuances, so little time. Tull really never stood still long enough for anybody to get a bead on them, for better or worse. But the day radio stopped playing one side or other of *Aqualung* is the moment that the dynamic "Locomotive Breath" swept forth to prove what a dramatic proposition Ian Anderson and his merry men could be when they felt like it.

CRM: 1:24—The Richter needle goes off the scale. Another earthquake? No, just the first thud of the bass line.

60. The Who—"Pinball Wizard" (1969)

Visually it's hard to disassociate *Tommy*'s greatest hit from the scene in the movie, with the hyper-platformed Elton John leading the band through a manic reconstruction of the deaf, dumb, and blind boy's most potent anthem. But musically, the original is still the one that matters.

CRM: 0:25—The first crash of electric thunder.

61. Free—"All Right Now" (1970)

A transatlantic Top 5 smash in 1970, "All Right Now" rode what has become one of the most instantly recognizable riffs in rock history, tied to one of the most universally familiar scenarios—"your average bloke chatting up your average chick," as vocalist Paul Rodgers put it. "Timeless."

CRM: 2:10—Paul Kossoff's tight solo ushers in a world of air guitar heroes.

62. Norman Greenbaum—"Spirit in the Sky"

It's the guitar tone that makes the song what it is, a snorting, snuffling, infectious fuzz that is so wholly divorced from the lyric that it's easy to see why so many bands have been trying to rewrite it ever since.

CRM: 2:02—The moment the guitar solo swaggers in over the riff.

63. Kansas—"Carry On Wayward Son"

One of the few genuinely credible American prog bands, Kansas sounded a little too close to Yes for a lot of European listeners. But "Carry On Wayward Son" had a tousled insouciance that lifted it above the bulk of the band's fare.

CRM: 0:20—The crunch of the band crashing over the opening harmonies.

64. Steppenwolf—"Magic Carpet Ride"

Another of those records that sounds a helluva lot funkier today than we noticed at the time, and a lot less gutsy as well. John Kay sounds like he's reading a shopping list, and where the harmonies should shout, they merely mumble. But what the hell, it's an acid rock classic.

CRM: 4:08—A driving organ and effects solo looks set to bring this record to an end, and you know The Moment is coming up fast. And then, mere seconds later, it's all over.

65. The Eagles—"Witchy Woman"

Spectral enough to merit its title, and haunted by one of the Eagles' most memorable guitar lines, "Witchy Woman"'s somber saga of a California cokehead could have been about anyone. Really, anyone. But everybody had their own theories regardless.

CRM: 2:36—The Eagles' own "Bohemian Rhapsody" moment, courtesy of the Brothers Gibb.

66. King Crimson—"Epitaph"

One of the three indisputable classics that made Crimson's *In The Court of the Crimson King* debut so eternal ("21st Century Schizoid Man" and the title track are the others), the boiling percussion and psilocybic mellotrons of "Epitaph" coupled with Greg Lake's most guileless vocal to deliver foreboding dread into even the brightest heart. Years later, an entire musical genre would arise around "Epitaph"'s gothic sensibilities, but if silence couldn't drown the screams, then a box of dry ice and a drum machine certainly weren't going to.

CRM: 1:46—So effective that Greg Lake continued to use it long after he left King Crimson, as a moment of drama during ELP's "Tarkus."

67. The Doors—"Riders on the Storm"

Nobody singing Morrison's poetic praises is likely to pick this one as proof of his genius; indeed, it packs some of the cheesiest lyrics he ever created. But the atmosphere is unimpeachable and, if you catch the version on the *American Prayer* collection, there's a spoken-word intro that actually allows you to forgive everything. Even the bit about the toad. Be honest: Have you *ever* seen a toad squirming?

CRM: 1:42—The first instrumental break, preceded by that chilling "yeaaaaaaaaaaahhhh."

68. The Who—"Baba O'Reilly"

Opening *Who's Next*, it was Pete Townshend's little joke, titling one of his most raucous compositions at least in part for a guru who had long ago taken a vow of silence. But "Baba [Meher] O'Reilly" fits the scenario regardless, a bitter remonstration toward a society that seemed hell-bent on hanging an entire generation of kids out to rot. Debuting the fevered whiplash of synth and guitar that would be reused to such effect in the same album's closing "Won't Get Fooled Again," "Baba O'Reilly" also ushered in one of Townshend's most potent slogans: "It's only teenage wasteland."

CRM: 1:48—Another of those classic Townshend moments, a chord that scythes through everything. But you could also choose Moonie's first drum break (2:33), or even Daltrey's realization that "they're all wasted" (3:29). Basically, the song is full of them.

69. Joe Walsh—"Rocky Mountain Way"

A guitar that swaggers as high as the Rockies, a vocal sucking oxygen from the rarefied air, and a riff that positively skis down the slope, "Rocky Mountain Way" blew off Walsh's delightfully titled *The Smoker You Drink, the Player You Get* LP in 1973, and you could still hear it rocking through the *Hotel California* three years later. Plus, think what it did for Peter Frampton! You heard the talk box here first, folks.

CRM: 1:10—It's the way the chorus comes swaggering in! Priceless.

70. Steve Miller Band—"Journey from Eden"

Proof that there was a lot of life before "The Joker" and all (don't worry, they're coming up), the Miller Band's most gorgeously understated epic.

CRM: 1:19—The first of the tempo shifts that really don't change anything. But the mood takes a shift to the left regardless.

71. Argent—"Hold Your Head Up"

One of *the* shock hit singles of the early 1970s, regardless of Rod Argent's past in the Zombies, a lurching, loose organ/chant workout that just happened to pack a killer chorus.

CRM: 4:14—A split second of almost absolute deathly silence that surprises you every time.

72. Deep Purple—"Child in Time"

In its original studio incarnation, "Child in Time" was regarded as among the most potent, and poignant, of all British rock commentaries on the then-ongoing Vietnam War, and survived to become a private anthem for many of the underground opposition groups forged by the political turmoil in 1980–90s Eastern Europe. To truly appreciate its chilling dynamics, seek out the version on the live *Made in Japan*, Gillan soaring to unimaginable heights, note for garroted note, and the ricochet never gets dull.

CRM: 2:27—Why is this man screaming?

73. Jimi Hendrix—"All Along the Watchtower"

Most people had barely cracked the shrink-wrap around Dylan's *John Wesley Harding* when the Jimi Hendrix Experience lifted "All Along the Watchtower" and released it as a single in time for the Tet Offensive. As Vietnam burned and the American military reeled from the shock, Hendrix spoke for everyone who wondered how a simple peacekeeping operation had ever come to this. "None of them along the line know what any of this is worth," he condemned. "There must be *some* way out of here."

CRM: 0:53—The first of the solos, although this is another of those records that just bristles with heart-stopping moments. They don't make records like this anymore.

74. Mountain—"Mississippi Queen"

A live leviathan, it could have been recorded with a little more finesse, but it still captures the essence of New York's heaviest trio.

CRM: 1:43—The first burst of incoherence at the end of the solo.

75. The Eagles—"One of These Nights"

That burbling bass intro is so laid back that it could be horizontal. But Don Felder's multitracked guitar won't let it relax, and though you suspect the rock is too soft (and the harmonies are still doing that Bee Gee thing they used to love so much), there's just enough of a frantic edge to keep things moving.

CRM: 2:20—Felder lets fly.

76. Led Zeppelin—"Immigrant Song"

It's no secret that Heart took more than the occasional liberty with Zeppelin. But did you know they also took the riff of "Immigrant Song" for their second album's "Barracuda"?

CRM: 0:10—The wordless wail that kicks it all off.

77. Van Morrison—"St. Dominic's Preview"

Cut so firmly in the spirit of the Stones' *Let It Bleed/Sticky Fingers* apogee that it's hard sometimes to tell the two apart.

CRM: 1:03—It's a long way to Buffalo!

78. Steve Miller Band—"The Joker"

Miller's first major hit in 1973 was the culmination of eleven years of nonstop touring. "It was like I knew every vaudeville hall in the United States, and was playing each one of them three times a year. Then *The Joker* happened: We had just finished a sixty-city tour and were just starting another one—that's the way we booked them. 'The Joker' was the number one record in the country, and we were playing 3,000-seat halls." It was insane, it was exhausting, and he celebrated by dropping out of sight for the next close-to-two years.

CRM: 0:18—Some people reckon they can make their guitar speak. But how many can make it wolf whistle?

79. Neil Young—"Cinnamon Girl"

As wild as it is brief, this was the glorious multi-guitar extravaganza that kicked Young's second album, *Everybody Knows This Is Nowhere*, into gear. Typically, the rest of the set was nowhere near as ebullient.

CRM: 2:07—See your baby start dancing!

80. Mountain—"Nantucket Sleighride"

Prefaced by a lilting minute of the instrumental "Taunta," but cross-faded to render the two inseparable, Mountain's mightiest moment is not merely the greatest song about whale hunting ever written (although it is). It also packs some of the most scintillating guitar-organ interplay this side of Purple, and leaves you wondering why everything the band did could not have been this timeless.

CRM: 2:43—British readers of a certain age will recognize it as the theme to television's *Weekend World*. For the rest of the planet it's one of the most dramatic riffs never to be given the free rein it deserves.

81. Lou Reed—"Walk on the Wild Side"

With Reed still recovering from the Velvet Underground, and with one failed solo set already behind him, Lou's label, RCA, really weren't expecting miracles when he went into the studio with David Bowie, in early 1972. In fact, they got two of the things: a magnificent album, *Transformer*, and a single that seemed to get bigger and bigger, the more people did a double take at the lyrics. And the colored girls say, "Doo-doo-doo . . . ."

CRM: 1:03—Positively the first hit record *not* to disguise fellatio beneath some line of clever innuendo.

82. Foghat—"Slow Ride" (1975)

Having broken out of the latest breakup to sunder Savoy Brown, Foghat were already five albums and hundreds of live shows old when they delivered their signature tune. But the blistering blues churner epitomized everything that everyone loved about the band. Plus, you've got to adore a song that starts with its chorus. And then keeps running with it.

CRM: 2:15—A moment of silence, and then the song keeps on going.

83. Kiss—"Detroit Rock City"

Half Kiss magnificence, half Bob Ezrin madness, Kiss' *Destroyer* album remains the band's most potent statement of intent, and the one that they best lived up to, too. Convoluted intro notwithstanding, "Detroit Rock City" captures everything they ever meant, louder and lewder than ever before.

CRM: 1:36—Here comes ACE!

84. Grand Funk—"We're an American Band"

The title track from Grand Funk's ninth album in four years (and their first since lopping the railroad off their name), "We're an American Band" might have been the most redundant statement of the age, but it was also one of the most glorifyingly affirmative. "We're coming to your town, we'll help you party down." Not as purposefully heavy as some of the band's earlier material, it became the group's chart-topping single, and laid down the law for every touring band of the next three years.

CRM: 0:09—The moment you realize that it's not going to be one long drum solo.

85. Juicy Lucy—"Who Do You Love?"

Noodles on crack! Stepping out of the marooned remnants of California's Misunderstood, Juicy Lucy debuted with positively the most sinister Bo Diddley cover ever conceived. Breakneck guitars seethe and steam, the dirt track smokes, and when you slit open the belly of the crocodile, a stack of Marshall amps tumble out. The bayou has never sounded so black.

CRM: 1:16—The moment the guitar stops screaming and the swamp snake steps back to the mic.

86. Bob Seger—"Night Moves"

Lurching from Motor City Madman to Detroit's answer to Van Morrison, with a touch of the Springsteens thrown into the street balladry, Seger nevertheless nails the nostalgic teen anthem bang between the eyes.

CRM: 2:35—You gotta love the way those backing vocals come chiming in, riding the back of the drumbeat.

87. Black Oak Arkansas—"Jim Dandy to the Rescue"

Lavern Baker scored the original hit with the song, and she delivered it with such a sly smile that it rarely raised its head above the novelty bunker. But Jim "Dandy" Mangrum reclaimed it and, with the stunning Ruby Starr on guest squeaks and exhortations, transformed it into a breakneck statement of defiant braggadocio.

CRM: 0:14—Go, Jim Dandy, go!

88. Neil Young—"Southern Man"

Hard-core addicts go for the side-long rendition on *4 Way Street*, but the regular studio take packs just as much power, and a more economical guitar solo, too.

CRM: 1:20—It clatters and crashes through the first verse and chorus, and then everything crashes together for the bridge.

89. ZZ Top—"Tush"

Wriggling out from beneath one of the most distinctive guitar tones in rock, the li'l ol' boogie band from Texas head downtown, and we all know what they're looking for.

CRM: 0:50—Billy Gibbons' duck-walk guitar just sends you swinging across the floor.

90. Bad Company—"Can't Get Enough" (1974)

A solid return to vocalist Paul Rodgers' Free-filled past, after even he had veered away from its most earthy joys, "Can't Get Enough" wasn't quite a rewrite of "All Right Now."

But the riff was almost as brutal, the solo was almost as breathtaking, and the song remains a kick-ass reminder of all the promise that Bad Company evinced when they first appeared. Shame that it all went so wrong.

CRM: 0:04—They count it in and BANG. Perfection!

91. T. Rex—"Bang a Gong"

The UK title, "Get It On," was apparently considered too raunchy for Stateside consumption, but chorus and verse leave you in no doubt as to the song's true intent, while Bolan's vision of girls, cars, and girls-as-cars remains as impossibly romantic as it ever was. Backing vocals by Flo and Eddie Turtle, incidentally.

CRM: 0:40—The first go-round for that inviolate chorus.

92. Heart—"Magic Man"

The Zeppelin comparisons fell like rain, but they meant absolutely nothing when confronted with this, lascivious, slippery, and sultry as hell, and all underpinned by that impossibly fluid guitar.

CRM: 3:53—And just when you think it's all over . . .

93. Thin Lizzy—"The Boys Are Back in Town"

"The Boys Are Back in Town" is *the* crucial Thin Lizzy song, not because it's their best (although it might be), or their most memorable (although it could be), but because it captured a moment in time so perfectly that, like "All You Need Is Love" in 1967, or "School's Out" in 1972, it's *impossible* to recall the summer of 1976 without that jukebox in the corner blasting out your favorite songs.

CRM: 1:06—If you really want to be a stickler for detail, it's the opening chord. But hold on for a minute and that little guitar refrain's a killer as well.

94. Kinks—"Lola"

If it didn't ignite Britain's glam rock fascination, Ray Davies' super-coy ode to gender-bending was certainly present at its birth, even if half of its listeners were still scratching their heads about it long after the fact.

CRM: 2:57—The sheer exuberance with which Davies relates that final verse provokes more sing-alongs than any other record on this list. I know what I am, and I bet I'm a man . . . and so was Lola. Oops.

95. Humble Pie—"Walk on Gilded Splinters" (live)

From the epochal *Rockin' the Fillmore* album, Dr. John's finest hour drawn out for almost half an hour, and a showcase for everything that made Pie so tasty. Deep and dangerous, it's the sort of performance that hangs in the corner of your darkened bedroom, waiting for that moment when you finally close your eyes . . . and then it pounces. Chicken bones not included.

CRM: 4:41—You've walked through the fire, flown through the smoke, and here comes the chorus like shivers down your spine

96. Steve Miller Band—"Fly Like an Eagle"

Miller's first solid shot at the commercial gold ring and it was a hole in one, no question. Still one of the most absurdly likeable albums ever made, and home to a host of hit singles, *Fly Like an Eagle* is nevertheless dominated by its title track, all bubbling synths and breathy boys, while everything percolates furiously beneath.

CRM: 3:27—Shades of Lou Reed's "Walk on the Wild Side," doo-doo-doo-doo-doo!

97. Creedence Clearwater Revival—"I Heard It Through the Grapevine"

A classic song, but this is the definitive rendition, as swampy and sexy as Marvin always meant it to sound (but Motown wouldn't let him), shot through with a bass line that just won't let go. Too much of Creedence's reputation is based upon what they *should* have sounded like, as opposed to what they really did accomplish. This one bottles up all their seething, livid promise.

CRM: 3:10—The moment the guitar rises out of the bayou.

98. Alice Cooper—"School's Out"

Teenage perversity of the first degree, "School's Out" is an emphatic celebration of what? The end of term? The end of the year? The end of institutionalized education as we know it? Nobody knew, but the sight of Cooper and his cronies whipping it up on prime-time TV was enough to outrage even the most liberal sensibilities. A few years later, Johnny Rotten was hired by the Sex Pistols on the strength of being able to mime to this song.

CRM: 0:44—Or is it that very last day before vacation begins? School's out!

99. James Gang—"Walk Away"

Another of those riffs that says so much that it's almost a shame there's a lyric to distract from it. But that chorus! It might be shorter than it has any right to be, but once heard, it's never forgotten.

CRM: 1:30—Walsh's guitar takes central stage. Of course it does.

100. Thin Lizzy—"Jailbreak"

"Jailbreak" is pure poetry in its vision, but its beauty is sprayed like graffiti across the riffs, cutting into the performance with the band already in full flood, laying out its warning in half-hushed tones of conspiracy and confidence. . . .

CRM: 2:18— . . . and then letting loose all hell, in the shape of solos and sirens, with the self-fulfilling cry of "Breakout!"

Note: Beatles, individually and collectively, were purposefully omitted from this list, partly because they might otherwise have consumed the entire one hundred, but also because there still wouldn't have been room for them all. Honorary mentions, however, to more or less the entire contents of Lennon's *Imagine* and *Sometime in New York City*, McCartney's *Band on the Run* and *Venus and Mars*, hits collections by George and Ringo, and just about the whole of the "white album." Nothing from *Sgt. Pepper*, though.

Bubbling Under, or, Just a Little Bit Too Late

AC/DC—"Back in Black"
AC/DC—"Highway to Hell"
Alice Cooper—"I'm 18"
Cliff Richard—"Devil Woman"
Fleetwood Mac—"Tusk"
Grand Funk Railroad—"The Locomotion"
Jethro Tull—"Aqualung"
Led Zeppelin—"Since I've Been Loving You"
Lou Reed—"Street Hassle"
Neil Young—"Like a Hurricane"
Neil Young—"Rust Never Sleeps"
Nils Lofgren—"Back It Up"
Pink Floyd—"Not Now, John"
Queen—"Another One Bites the Dust"
Queen—"We Are the Champions"
Rolling Stones—"Start Me Up"
Rush—"Tom Sawyer"
Steely Dan—"Rikki, Don't Lose That Number"
Tom Petty & the Heartbreakers—"American Girl"
Yes—"Roundabout"

ACKNOWLEDGMENTS

A LOT OF PEOPLE THREW A LOT OF OPINIONS into this book, most of which were promptly thrown back out again. Yes, thank you for sending me a list of your Top 20 Twisted Sister B-sides, but I really don't care. But Amy Hanson suffered more than most as this volume took shape and the drilling in the wall grew louder, and I'd also like to thank Jo-Ann Greene for the immortal rejoinder, "I'm sorry, but the Eagles aren't classic rock, they're shit." Veronique cheer-led loudly for Rush, but I forgot to listen to her, and my editor, Mike Edison, had serious issues with the inclusion of Fleetwood Mac, but I forgot to listen to him as well.

Thanks also to Jenny and James, Linda and Larry, Phil and Paula (why do so many of my closest friends sound like late '50s pop duos?), Sue and Tim, Deb and Roger, Bob and Jane, Chris and Amy Beth, Gaye and Tim, Dave and Sue. Oliver, Toby, and Trevor (at last, a late '50s folk trio). Jenny W.; Karen T.; Anchorite Man; Bateerz and family; Chrissie Bentley; Blind Pew; Mrs. B. East; J. D.; Mrs. Nose and family; Gef the Talking Mongoose; the Gremlins who live in the heat pump; Geoff Monmouth; Naughty Miranda; Nutkin; Steve, for remembering his own period favorites; a lot of Thompsons; and Neville Viking. This note's for you.

Who wants originality?
I know who don't, yeah that's me
All new music is a bore,
just need what I've heard before

—The Lurkers, "Come and Reminisce"